A CANAL AND WATERWAYS ARMCHAIR BOOK

JOHN GAGG

with line drawings by Robert Wilson
and photographs by the author

DAVID & CHARLES
NEWTON ABBOT LONDON
NORTH POMFRET (VT) VANCOUVER

Other books by John Gagg

THE CANALLERS' BEDSIDE BOOK
Canals in Camera—1
Canals in Camera—2
5000 Miles, 3000 Locks
John Gagg's Book of Locks

for children

Rivers in Britain
Boats and Boating
Boats and Ships

ISBN 0 7153 7057 x
Library of Congress Catalog Card Number 75–10613

Set in 12 on 13 Bembo
and printed in Great Britain
at the Alden Press, Oxford
for David & Charles (Publishers) Limited
Brunel House Newton Abbot Devon

Published in the United States of America
by David & Charles Inc
North Pomfret Vermont 05053 USA

Published in Canada
by Douglas David & Charles Limited
132 Philip Avenue North Vancouver BC

PREFACE

When I was writing *The Canallers' Bedside Book* there was not the space for all my collection of canal items. The title also excluded intriguing aspects of the navigable rivers linked with our canals. Here, then, is a companion book which not only adds to the canal snippets, but also roams along the Nene and the Trent, the Avon and the Great Ouse, and several other rivers of character.

Again I hope it is a book for the reader with a sense of humour as well as an interest in waterways. It is often light-hearted, but not without serious waterway purpose too. I look at bottled gas as well as at the British Waterways Board, at shearpins and at Galton Tunnel, at badgers and at coal-carrying, at canal cowboys and at tunnel-legging, at Potter Heigham bridge and at the magnificent Avon restoration.

Again, too, you don't have to start at the beginning, for it is a book for dipping into. Nor, of course, need you be in an armchair, for it is also usable in bed or bunk.

I might add, perhaps, that books such as this could not be written without the aid of waterway-enthusiast crews, who wind up the paddles and watch the ropes and even fetch take-away meals while I'm busy with camera or dictating machine. So my thanks to my own keen helpers, especially, recently, Andrew Vicary.

JOHN GAGG

Alrewas

This village on the Trent & Mersey Canal has no spectacular claim to waterway fame, and merely starts off this book by alphabetical accident. All the same, it is worth mentioning for several reasons.

At the time of writing, for example, two very well-known waterway experts happen to live there—one now editing a waterway magazine, and the other applying his talents to a range of waterway activities, journalistic, photographic, technical and architectural. Thus I rarely pass through Alrewas

5

without a friendly chat—and indeed, on two occasions, rapidly-answered calls for assistance.

Alrewas also sits on a curious bit of waterway engineering, in that the Trent runs into the canal for a short distance, and then hastily out again. This must help to keep the water-level happy all the way down to Shardlow, but in times of flood it can make navigation a tricky business, and you are better advised to stay above Alrewas lock if the river below it is raging fiercely. Normally, however, you travel through into unusally deep water and make your way to Wychnor lock, and then on to that dreary stretch beside the A38.

I'm told that road travellers find Alrewas dull and characterless. But the canal and river area around the church is attractive, with quiet moorings and only a short walk to one of the handiest shopping-places for many canal miles. Further on you can go aground if you swing too widely by the recreation ground when approaching the upper (Bagnall) lock; and the brickwork of the bridge entering this lock is alarmingly worn now by generations of boats, while the balance-beams of the bottom gates must be among the shortest in the system. Once through though, you are on a pleasant lonely stretch before the Piccadilly Circus of Fradley Junction.

Better to moor the night at Alrewas, anyhow—unless, as once happened to me, somebody leaves a paddle up, and you wake in the morning with a list.

Anton's Gowt

This is an odd enough item, and I'm sorry I don't know who Anton was, or what exactly a Gowt is. But anyone who has braved the long, long haul down the Witham towards Boston will have seen the place of this name.

On a windy bend just before the long-awaited last lap on this bleak river, it is marked by a low house on the bend which has been in sight for some time. By the house is a bridge sideways on to the Witham, and, lo and behold, a lock under the bridge. This (the lock? the house? the place?) is Anton's Gowt.

River Avon: lock gear

Borrowing a key from the house, you can pass through the lock and into the weird water world of the Witham Navigable Drains. They meander almost as much as the Birmingham Canal Navigations, though there are no tunnels, there is only one other usable lock, and there aren't as many miles of water. But they amble hither and thither, up West Fen Drain and down Newham, along Castle Dyke and Lush's, by West Fen Catchwater and Cowbridge. And through the smart-looking guillotined Cowbridge lock you can travel on Maud Foster's Drain and moor in the heart of Boston, much more pleasantly than if you had continued down the open Witham.

You may find that there isn't enough water in the Drains to float you, especially in the spring, but if you have a shallow draught, and a low roof, you can spend many adventurous hours getting thoroughly lost in these mysterious Fenland backwaters.

Avon River

This is the Warwickshire one, and it now holds a glorious place
in the history of inland waterways in this century. There have
been many restorations of derelict waterways, large and small,
with the southern Stratford Canal being a highlight in 1964, and
the Kennet & Avon struggling through to offer an even more
spectacular revival one day. But the upper River Avon has an
astonishing story in several ways.

The Avon's history, like that of so many navigations, has been
a sad tale, with the upper river under railway ownership
becoming totally unnavigable in the 1870s, and the lower river
below Evesham remaining only in erratic use. The Lower Avon
Navigation Trust brought its part of the river back into full use
by 1964, but the upper part remained a challenging gap in the
waterway map. If this gap could be closed, not only would the
Midland waterways have a new link to the Severn and the sea,
but a delightful ring of cruising waters would be opened. The
end of the restored Stratford Canal needed joining in this way

8

to the restored Lower Avon, and this was a job crying out to be done.

And of course one man's name came to mind—David Hutchings, the Stratford Canal restorer and a name to conjure with in getting things done, even at the expense of putting a few backs up. So with an anonymous £100,000, subscribing 'foundationers', and even collecting-boxes in pubs, and with vigorous waterway campaigner Robert Aickman as chairman, the Upper Avon Navigation Trust set to work.

The old locks were heaps of rubble, so nine brand new sites were planned, and locks were invented which looked like no other locks anywhere else on the waterways. Many volunteers, prisoners and later Borstal boys streamed along to the task. Gates and gear were begged from elsewhere, and ingenious devices brought into use to open the gates—including old Thames capstans lying on their sides. And these new locks often include a far greater number of helpful bollards, ladders and landing stages than most long-standing locks on other long-used waterways.

No doubt somebody will write the story of this achievement one day, including the obstinacy of official bodies, and the remarkable financial meanness of councils which could receive nothing but benefit from the restoration. There was outright opposition to the whole idea in some quarters, and the Trust was forced to carry out a tremendous amount of extra work—especially dredging—to meet a string of surprising conditions imposed upon it. Even Stratford-upon-Avon looked coldly on the project as it had looked coldly on the canal ten years earlier. Yet nowadays the colourful boats at Stratford draw almost as much tourist attention as the clattering tills of Shakespeariana—probably the only free attraction in Stratford.

The Avon now is a magnificent cruise. It is in fact navigable for a few miles above Stratford, and it runs down also through these fine new locks and amid weeping willows among remote countryside. Luddington village lurks behind trees, but Bidford sits on the river—though offering little welcome in the way of moorings. Indeed, a lack of moorings is the only blot on both upper and lower Avon. Evesham tries to push boats discreetly out of the way well below the main bridge, and with absurd warnings against hanging laundry on deck. Pershore offers better moorings, but they are now quite inadequate, while a further stretch forbids boats to tie up.

Despite these quaint implications that boaters are not quite nice to have around, thousands of perfectly ordinary decent people now enjoy a cruise down a delightful river, from Stratford to sophisticated Tewkesbury and the Severn. Thank you, both Upper and Lower Navigation Trusts.

Aylesbury Arm

Curiously this was one of the last lengths of canal that I explored—probably because I live within a few miles of it. It takes a strong-willed decision for anyone on the Grand Union to cruise down there, however, for he is committing himself to a return journey of 32 locks, merely to travel just over 6 miles to a dead end. Moreover, he is liable to meet some very shallow and narrow pounds in the process.

For some reason Aylesbury basin has become a sort of Mecca for full-sized narrow boats—the very vessels which find the greatest difficulty in navigating the Arm. Some famous boats—*Pearl*, for example—carry or have carried 'Aylesbury' on their sides, and how on earth they manoeuvre down there when there is a full house I have yet to see. All the same, like the ascent of Everest, the journey is one that every serious canaller ought to attempt, merely in order to have done it.

Unlike the Grand Union broad locks, the Aylesbury Arm locks are narrow, and the top two offer an immediate surprise by being in the form of a staircase, seemingly unknown to most writers and guides. If you commit the usual gaffe of emptying a full top lock into a full bottom one, the water mercifully pours over the rather lower bottom gate. Then the Arm is curiously isolated, and steps its way down through lonely fields, with hardly a building nearby until Aylesbury itself begins to appear.

Even there you slip quietly in, and suddenly realise that you

are almost under the shadow of the unusually tall County Hall. Let us hope you have room to turn round then, for the terminus itself has been dominated recently by a huge new concrete building which cuts off the former view of the canal from the Wendover road. The shops are only a few minutes away, however, if you can get out of the basin. And if you don't want to shop, you can still find several widely experienced canal users to talk to on some of the boats moored there.

Then of course you have the 16 locks back up again. If you want to spend any time in historic but traffic-cluttered Aylesbury, you'll need to allow the whole day for the return trip on the Arm.

Badgers

One of the pleasures of cruising inland is that you see many creatures and flowers rarely seen by less fortunate mortals. Kingfishers, if your eye is quick, wagtails, mallards, moorhens, coots and swans are among the birds, and there are always water-voles plopping under and cunning pike lurking below overhanging bushes. I once saw a very surprised fox trotting on the towpath after dark one snowy evening along the northern Oxford. Badgers are probably the rarest sight you'll see.

11

This is not because the badgers themselves are rare—in fact there are surprising numbers of them—but they hardly ever come out in the daytime, preferring to sleep in their underground homes when everyone else is about. They are the biggest wild animals we have apart from deer, with remarkably good senses of smell and hearing, though their eyesight is not up to much. Their habits and lives are well worth studying, and they could give us lessons in keeping our own environment tidy. Your best chance of seeing a badger is to moor in a lonely area and keep your eyes and ears open after dark. You may hear the curious scream that badgers sometimes give and if this doesn't scare you, and you keep still enough, you may see one slinking along looking for slugs and snails, roots and worms, beetles and even small animals. Badgers are quite good at eating wasp grubs, too, and they take no notice of the wasps buzzing around.

The saddest sight, though, is a badger when it has drowned in the water. Once in a steep-sided channel, and especially in a lock, it cannot get out again. I recently saw one lying on a balance-beam at Swarkestone after someone had removed its body from the lock.

I can dine out for the rest of my life, however, on my chief encounter with a badger in a canal, for this one was still alive. I was moored on the Gloucester-Sharpness, and the sides of this canal are deep and vertical. At three o'clock one morning there was obviously something scrabbling about under the boat, so I had to go out and see what it was. I could see two paws in the moonlight, so I bent down and grabbed them, only to have one finger savagely bitten. But by holding the boat away with one foot I could give a heave and throw the animal ashore. And astonishingly, it was a badger. He didn't look very happy, but I left him to it while I sought first aid.

He was gone in the morning, but it was months before I had a new finger-nail. I can't blame him, though. I daresay I'd have felt the same if I'd been on the point of drowning in the Gloucester-Sharpness Ship Canal.

Birmingham

I have written of the pleasures of the Birmingham Canal Navigations in *The Canallers' Bedside Book*, and the fascinations of this Venice of the Midlands have lately received both welcome and unwelcome publicity. But I wish to commend here the remarkable waterway approach to the centre of Birmingham along the Birmingham & Fazeley Canal.

This is a route shunned by many, in favour of the level run in from Wolverhampton or that from King's Norton past the university. But the approach from Salford Junction is one of the most spectacular three miles of canal to be found anywhere—if you don't mind 24 locks.

It starts rather quietly, leaving the motorway bridges behind and passing between factory walls, with little warning of the climb to come. Even the first three locks are spaced out and secret, with only the second one having access to the outside world. This one also has a curious humped footbridge at its bottom end, cantilevered to allow a towing rope through under one end. There is also a cave-like recess in the widened road bridge to let the balance beam swing.

After this gentle start, and beyond the third lock, you suddenly see a pile of locks stacked up in front of you, just like a staircase. There is hardly a soul in sight as you clamber up, though obviously a wealth of manufacturing is going on all around you. But this 11-lock Aston flight passes lost among gasworks and mysterious vast new buildings before coming to a junction with the route from the Grand Union.

Take a breath now as you bear right under the A38 bridge, with a half-mile level before the Farmer's Bridge 13 locks. They are really memorable, for they are mostly straddled by massive buildings on concrete stilts, and the curiously-shaped Post Office tower dominates the whole of this final climb. You can hit some of the stilts very easily if there is a cross wind, for they have left little room for longer boats to manoeuvre, and the locks are so close that the pounds between extend sideways into hidden concrete caves.

The locks are easy to work, and the strange contrast between the almost complete silence and the obvious dominance of the city nearby is uncanny. You pass through tunnels—like Snow Hill—and out into the open again, and all the time you are quite unable to reach this other world outside your route. It is not until you emerge from the top lock that you suddenly find contact with people once more. Even then, when you cross to the much-publicised *Long Boat*, you may find yourself climbing the railings because the little gate at the end is so well disguised.

But you have arrived in Birmingham, and you can actually make your way out of this secret waterway world and into the pleasures or horrors of the traffic-ridden city.

The historic Gas Street Basin round the corner seems now almost as busy with trip boats as the city centre is with cars, and as a pleasant mooring is completely spoiled for passing canallers. Even the dwellers on the narrow boats there must find their haven now rudely disturbed. In fact it is sometimes almost as difficult to get through Worcester Bar as it was in the days when it was a solid barrier, which is a pity.

Bishop's Stortford

This is another of those many towns which for years ignored the navigations which are part of them. Perhaps now, as with other places, this may be changing as people realise what a pleasant amenity a river or a canal can be.

Bishop's Stortford is the furthest point you can reach by cruising up the River Lee from the heart of London and turning right into the more canal-like River Stort past Roydon, Harlow and Sawbridgeworth. These places on the route might also turn their attention to the river, for mooring is often difficult. Yet the locks and many of the stretches between are quite delightful, with a few remaining intriguing little lock-houses sporting Sir George Duckett's emblem.

The last lap towards Bishop's Stortford is especially relaxing, with boats moored on the arm to Little Hallingbury and many trees alongside the river. But once you enter the town the

15

surroundings deteriorate, and your cruise fizzles out without much warning beside a noisy car-park. Mooring is not easy, and the only advantage is that a few yards through the mass of cars brings you to handy supermarkets to stock up your larder. You may be tempted to visit the museum to Cecil Rhodes who was born here. But with a mill on one side of the river and the car park on the other, you may feel moved to go back into the country to moor for the night.

Bollards

I have written about bollards in general in *The Canallers's Bedside Book*, but I have since come across examples on the Lee and Stort which even out-bollard those beauties on the River Nene. Not only do the Lee and Stort provide massive metal ones at locksides, looking like square flat-topped mushrooms, but they

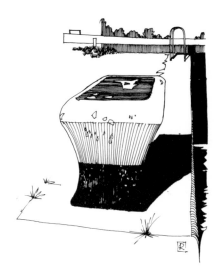

also offer small ones tucked into the walls of the locks.

I have seen the same thing at Gloucester, and presumably you are supposed to transfer your ropes as you rise or fall, though this seems to me an unnecessary and even hazardous business. It may perhaps be helpful in the deep Gloucester lock, but why it should be needed in the smaller and not-very-deep locks along the Lee and Stort I cannot imagine. The fine bollards on the locksides there could well be imitated elsewhere, but the lock-wall ones seem to be nothing more than decorative—unless I've missed the point.

Come to think about it, perhaps they could be removed and taken to the Nene, and placed above the locks there. For though the Nene has its fine lockside bollards, it hardly ever provides you with anything to tie to outside the top gates while you operate the paddles, except for one miserable bollard for your bows. This leaves your stern swinging unhappily about in the current. So any other spare bollards around the system would be thankfully received and placed about 70ft above the top gates on the Nene, for tying up sterns.

Bosley

I'm told you pronounce it Bose-ly, and it is worth mentioning as the name of an unusual flight of locks. They are unusual because the 12 of them together are the only locks on the whole of the Macclesfield Canal, apart from the entrance lock. Thus the Macc is like two level canals, 10 and 16 miles long, linked by about a mile of locks.

These locks are in fine countryside, with some woodland, wide views west and hills up east, and The Cloud—more than 1000ft up—looking down at you for some distance beforehand and as you start your way up the locks, just after crossing high over the River Dane.

You will be 110ft higher after the twelfth lock, where Bosley reservoir brings its water into the canal. There are some interesting stone steps up to the locksides and sturdy footbridges, but the unusual thing about the Bosley locks is that they have pairs of gates at their top ends as well as at the bottoms, whereas most narrow locks have a single gate at the top.

In all, it is a most enjoyable flight to pass through. The only thing I have against them is that I once collected a goodly length of barbed wire on my propeller just above the top lock, but I can hardly blame the locks for that.

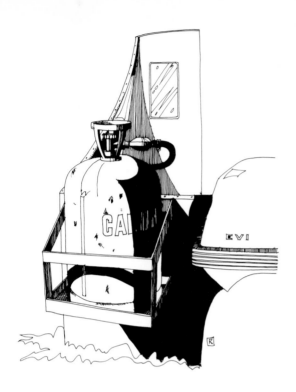

Bottled gas

This is one of the really vital constituents of waterway cruising. There are boats with paraffin or methylated spirit stoves, and all-year-round cruisers have solid fuel stoves; but the great majority rely on lumbering heavy metal liquid gas containers.

Gas has its dangers. It is heavier than air, so if it leaks it lies in your bilges, and more than one boat has been burnt out as a result. The Thames in particular has stringent regulations about gas fittings; all pipes, for example, must be visible. On all boats the bottles themselves should be either outside the boat or in a compartment sealed off from the rest of the boat and vented over the side so that leaking gas can escape harmlessly.

Cooker taps should always be carefully turned off, and the whole supply cut off at the bottle when not in use. Gas refrigerators are useful, but they too should be vented over the side, and should have a special cut-off device in case the burner flame is extinguished.

This all sounds alarming, but there is an ingenious gadget which you can fit in your bilges to sniff out the gas, and shout at you if it finds any. Or there are pumps which will remove gas and petrol fumes at the touch of a switch.

Using gas to heat a boat directly is not quite such a good idea as it seems, for the flame produces almost as much moisture as it produces heat, and the roof, sides and windows are soon streaming with water. My own particular gratitude to gas lies in an intriguing machine which I unearthed at a recent Boat Show, which throws out blasts of warm air all over the boat, while the moisture—or most of it—goes out through a flue.

Despite the dangers of gas, it is the boater's friend. But it has its infuriating moments; for example, the bottles tend to run out at awkward times. You can carry two bottles to be on the safe side, but I have even had them both empty at the same time. And to add insult to injury, it was Saturday night on the Coventry Canal in winter, just as a meal was cooking, so there was nothing left but to crawl into sleeping bags.

Small bottles are not too heavy to lug along to the nearest supplier for an exchange with full ones. But with large containers it is far better to take your boat as near to the replacements as possible, unless you want to be crippled for life carrying them.

Brecon & Abergavenny canal

I single out this canal for special mention because it is undoubtedly the most beautifully-situated route in the whole country. I see that British Waterways has started to call it the Monmouthshire & Brecon, after the 1865 amalgamation, but apart from a short silty length the canal now in use is the original Brecon & Abergavenny, so I shall stick to that title.

This magnificent waterway runs for 33 miles high up the hillsides above the Usk. For mile after mile you can look across

to mountains over what seems to be a sheer drop to the river below. Other hills and mountains tower above you and the whole area is within the Brecon Beacons National Park. Trees are with you always, making fantastic tunnels and reflecting their tracery in the water ahead. The towpath is an exceptionally fine one, and broad enough at times to look like a green road.

The views are always striking and sometimes spectacular. You can look down on the roofs of Abergavenny from the remarkably-sited boatyard at Llanfoist, and at the southern end of the canal the valley opens out until you seem to be looking down on an Ordnance Survey map, with beetles on the ribbons of roads.

In spring the welter of primroses, violets, cuckoo-flowers and bluebells is unbelievable; and of course it is then, too, that the colours on the trees show their greatest variety. You cruise along amid this eye-dazzling range of colour, hardly touching a village; yet within a short distance, most of the time, are friendly little pubs and shops.

The Brecon is not connected with the rest of the waterway system, and was in decay until the development of the National Park and the far-sighted financial help of the former Brecknock and Monmouth County Councils, which set examples that many other authorities could yet follow. Their contributions permitted channel clearance, bridge restoration, and towpath and hedge maintenance superior to that possible on most other canals, and with the provision of an interesting lift bridge at Talybont and a restored lock at Brynich, boats could reach Brecon again for the first time for many years.

The terminus is just a stone wall across the canal, which is a pity. And though obviously many visiting boats are brought on trailers from elsewhere, the waterway seems to see fewer craft than it deserves. Big boats would not be comfortable, especially under some of the bridges. But several cruiser hire firms operate along the canal, and any inland waterway enthusiast who has not tried the Brecon hasn't lived—even though its mere six locks may seem a very small ration after Tardebigge.

Bridges

I sometimes have the illusion that no two bridges along waterways are alike, but this cannot be so. Yet the variety of bridges, especially across canals, is quite remarkable. Admittedly individual canals often have their own particular styles—the solid, stone, almost horseshoe-shaped ones of the Macclesfield, and of course all those little split bridges on the Stratford, for example—but even then the styles seem to differ along different lengths of the same canal.

The Trent & Mersey, for one, has some mean bridges along its eastern part—mean for towed boats, anyhow, in that the horses often had to be uncoupled, since there are no towpaths beneath them. These bridges are usually at the foot of locks

(though there is an isolated one near Barton-under-Needwood) which even today can make the job of taking a boat in and out of the lock difficult (see STENSON). Yet at the other end of the Trent & Mersey the bridges are quite different, with several flat-girder-topped versions in the Weaver area looking far less penny-pinching than the brick arches of Derbyshire and Staffordshire.

Both the Leeds & Liverpool and the Lancaster have massive stone bridges, though in neither case do they curve in at the bottom like those on the Macclesfield, which are easier to steer a boat through than any bridges I know.

In contrast to this Macclesfield bridge-shape, canals such as the Oxford seem to specialise in lethal slopes, catching generations of cabin-tops so that the brickwork is heavily gouged. These quaint old bridges may be attractive to artists and photographers, but when they sag smartly towards the opposite field, boaters beware!

There are even flat-topped bridges lying in wait for cabin cruisers. One in particular in the Middle Level, crossed by the B660, is impassable if your top is 6ft above water at normal level. One is near Polesworth on the Coventry Canal which will sweep sunbathers—and maybe even flags, mops, shafts and ventilators—from your boat. The BCN has some treacherous bridges (usually those that have been strengthened by girders underneath), and you may set off up the Walsall Canal and never get out of the foot of Ryders Green locks. There is a nasty bridge going northwards into Stoke-on-Trent, whose bent girders look as if somebody had given it a hefty clout. And all those lift-bridges on the Oxford, the Llangollen, the Brecon, the Caldon and the northern Stratford will catch one side of your boat anyhow if you don't watch out—or if there is a cross-wind. Most of the time though, you clear bridges happily, but it is a foolish captain who allows sunbathing on his roof as he travels.

Dozens of odds and ends of bridges pass through my mind: there are those two double-arches, at Marton on the Leeds & Liverpool and in Grub Street cutting on the Shropshire Union; there is lofty Galton Bridge on the BCN, now almost hidden at one end by the new Galton tunnel (qv) and all those swing bridges on the Gloucester-Sharpness, with the keepers going round with their charges. Above Keadby lock on the Sheffield and South Yorkshire Navigation is that laborious railway sliding bridge and there is the awkward St John's Bridge at Tewkesbury, where you have to shoot through at such a sharp angle that it seems impossible to avoid hitting the bank.

As you cruise, you find yourself admiring so many of the bridges for their beauty, and constantly thinking of the surprising variety produced by the canal-builders in particular as they lifted thousands of roads and farm tracks over the channels. These bridges now make pleasing landmarks on our journeys—and indeed, their names and numbers are often the only clues to our location.

British Waterways

The majority of navigable waterways in Britain, and some no longer passable, are under the control of the British Waterways Board, commonly referred to as 'the Waterways' by their employees, 'the Board' in more formal terms, 'British Waterways' in usual circles and 'BW' hereunder.

Human nature being what it is, BW is frequently, but usually unfairly, criticised for shortcomings along the waterways it controls. Yet if any business had been starved of money in the way of BW, it would long since have gone bankrupt. The fact that BW canals and rivers are still as navigable as they are, despite having to be run on less than a shoestring, attracts far less praise than it ought.

On the surface, BW sometimes seems to invite the wrath of water users. It appears to allocate much money to glossy publicity, it puts up traditionalist backs by installing expensive new paddle-gear which cannot be checked from a distance, and it seems to close canals for surprisingly long periods for work which through layman's eyes could take much less time, or which ought not to cause a canal to be closed at all. This is especially irritating for the increasing numbers of people who pay for a 12-month licence and hope to travel at any time.

Its new waterway guides, too, annoyed many enthusiasts, for they were not the easiest things to read and the early issues fell to pieces rapidly. Moreover there are some curious antics in the lock-working diagrams, and I find the routes and descriptions to say the least confusing, with some of the text reading the opposite way to the journey.

Despite exasperations of this kind, criticism of BW and its ancestors was obviously unfair and absurd. Indeed the waterways associations should have directed attacks at politicians of all parties. BW suffered, and continues to suffer, from lack of financial support. While money is poured into other nationalised industries, our waterways have been expected almost to look after themselves; instead of being developed as a massive and money-saving transport system in their own right—as in other European countries—they have been allowed to run down until they could be sneered at as serving no useful purpose except leisure.

Yet leisure has now in itself become an important aspect of national policy and a little more money has flown into waterways recently, often from local councils rather than from central government.

But BW remains the poor relation of the nationalised boards, and it will do so until a far-sighted government realises that waterways are, and should be, transport highways. It is struggling to catch up with an almost impossible backlog of waterway maintenance. Above all, dredging is needed, yet any water user can see dredgers sitting idle. This and repairs to locks, tunnels, bridges and towpaths need millions of pounds, just to keep our waterways as they are at the moment. Vast new waterways would require heavier investment—yet still nothing like the increasingly wasteful cost of motorways.

No doubt our main road villages and towns will have to be knocked down by lorries, and traffic-jams stretch to Land's End, before anybody will really stir. But one day, by some miracle, BW may be given the money it needs to do the job it ought to be doing. And Britain might have a sensible modern waterways network used not only for transport or pleasure-boating but angling or just strolling along canal side paths. Meantime, don't blame BW for things that are not its fault. Stick to those that are.

Bunbury

Going up the Shropshire Union you find a sudden change of character after the fine embankment, aqueduct and basin at Nantwich. The fact is that you have left the straight Birmingham & Liverpool Junction Canal and entered the much older Chester Canal, broader and more winding. But 6 miles pass before you are more clearly reminded of this. Then you come to a pair of locks at Bunbury, and discover that they are twice as wide as the ones you have passed through so far. And just to rub in the point, they are in the form of a staircase.

Staircase locks run straight into each other without any plain canal between, and this can lead to problems if you empty a full lock into another full lock immediately below. Some staircases have safety devices to allow for mistakes, sometimes in the form of an overflow lip in the lower lock to let the surplus water get away before it floods over the sides, as at Botterham on the Staffs & Worcs, and Etruria on the Caldon.

Bunbury isn't like this, though. If the lower lock is already full, and you empty the top lock into it, the water rises over the sides and especially over the bottom gates. This is all very well unless there happens to be an innocent soul waiting under the bridge to come up through the locks. If so, he is liable to be shot out like a cork unless he is well secured. Nor will the owners of boats moored just below the bridge thank you for a flush of water.

As always with staircases, it is best to observe one simple rule: when you empty a lock, make sure that the lock below has plenty of room for the water. This often means that you empty the lower one (or more) first.

If you can take your attention from the Bunbury locks for a moment, you'll see some pleasant old canal stables, and an old warehouse now used for building boats.

Camping boats

One waterway phenomenon which nobody can miss if they

visit the Grand Union for very long is the great growth of narrow boats taking parties of youngsters in simple camping style. Schools, scouts and other youth organisations are making increasing use of these boats, and even in winter you will see them about—at least at weekends—and the firms concerned must have introduced many thousands of young people to the waterways.

The parties, and standards of boat handling vary greatly: some groups are obviously well disciplined, wear life-jackets religiously, and behave sensibly both on the boat and on land; others, unhappily, cause considerable annoyance to other waterway users. They scramble dangerously about the boats, pile themselves on top to block the steerer's view (and to be swept off at bridges), yell at each other much of the time, and are allowed transistors at full blast. At locks this kind of party can be the biggest nuisance of all.

Nobody seems to have told them to look out for boats coming the other way, and they will rush ahead with windlasses and prepare locks regardless. They swarm all over the gates and balance beams so that it would be little wonder if two or three were missing by the bottom of the Stoke Bruerne flight, for example.

When you see parties of this kind—and thank goodness they are rare—both the boat steerer and the adults ostensibly in charge always look slightly bewildered at what they have let themselves in for. Enthusiasm among the young is one thing; uncontrolled and seemingly uncontrollable excitement or even hooliganism on canals, and especially at a flight of locks, is quite another.

I don't know what sort of suggestions or rules are put out by the companies operating camping boats, but with the increasing numbers of such boats, they must do more than merely hire them out. They must accept responsibility for what happens along the waterway. For that matter, I have seen the boats breasted up along narrow stretches so that other boats are driven aground. And sometimes, at locks, there is the implication that they have some form of priority as if they were carrying cargo.

It would be a great pity if this excellent system of introducing youngsters to the water at low cost should be spoiled by increasing annoyance to others.

Canal cowboys

This is a term used to describe people in boats who ought not to be on canals at all. There are not many about, and perhaps the hard work of canal locks will always keep their numbers low. But they are an unfortunate import from the easier and more crowded waterways elsewhere.

The canal cowboy is quickly identified by his selfishness and antagonism towards others. Usually he moves much too rapidly with an over-large engine, damaging banks and moored boats, and causing havoc to meals in preparation. He is ruthless and destructive at locks and movable bridges, and often travels about armed with airguns, transistors and quantities of beer. He antagonises not only other boaters but the anglers whose lines he roars through, the landlords of canalside pubs, the keepers of canalside shops, unfortunate men trying to put in piling as he passes, and exasperated lock-keepers.

This fortunately thinly-spread group, tossing their rubbish and emptying their buckets in the hedgerows or staggering noisily back to their boats when others are asleep, belong to the wider tribe of waterway VANDALS, about which I write later.

Canoes

You will not spend long exploring waterways, afoot or afloat, without meeting a canoe or a flock of canoes. There are the tough canoeists who use rivers and swift weirs for their activities (and to whom British Waterways address long solemn notices at dangerous river-weirs), and there are the gentler canoeists who prefer the still canals.

The latter have to face locks, where they usually carry their canoes. But I once watched a solitary canoe use 56,000 gallons of

water per lock as it moved up the Buckby flight. If a canoeist doesn't like locks he can try the Brecon, Lancaster or Fossdyke Canals, or some of the longer pounds elsewhere.

Canoeing is usually a day-trip exercise, carried out with the aid of a car roof-rack. But you will also meet determined youngsters in canoes loaded with camping gear, tackling extended waterway cruises. Larger boats usually slow down to pass canoes, only to be disconcerted as the paddler heads deliberately for their wash, and obviously enjoys being tossed about in it.

Caravans

Caravans have many affinities with boats and waterways, but in one way they are vitally different from boats, quite apart from having wheels. The essential difference is that you live in your boat as it moves along, you walk about in it and even cook and eat meals, as well as sleep, if you're in such a great hurry. But while a caravan is on the move you are not in it, but sitting uncomfortably in the seat of a car.

You can use a caravan only when it is moored, as it were. Moreover, your boat (in most places) travels in far less crowded conditions than your car and caravan—though admittedly the wheels have a greater choice of routes, and you can leave a caravan at times and still get about. All the same, even the most ardent caravanner wouldn't pretend that towing a caravan along today's roads is as leisurely an activity as cruising in a boat along rivers and canals.

31

Caravans and boats, however, are similar in one particular aspect: they each have to make the greatest use of their space in ingenious ways. Tables and seats turn into beds, there are scaled-down cookers, sinks, wash-basins and lavatories, cunning cupboards and partitions, and all sorts of other quart-into-pint-pot ideas can be found in both boats and caravans. Most boaters at some time or other find themselves having a peep round caravan showrooms. Caravans have a space advantage in that their sides are vertical and their bottoms are flat, but boats can stretch themselves to 70ft long to make up for this.

Each to his taste, however. As you cruise along canals and especially rivers it is fairly obvious that many caravan enthusiasts feel drawn to the water, too. Along the Severn and Avon, the Nene and Great Ouse, the Staffs & Worcs Canal and the Macclesfield you can sometimes spot whole caravan villages or even small towns. They line up in neat ranks close to the water, and often have their dinghies and inflatables moored to the bank.

One of the most extensive yet well-spaced caravan towns is near Billing lock on the Nene. It has vast stretches of neatly-mown grass, and very polite inhabitants who will come and chat with you as you slowly raise the guillotine.

Many riverside caravans of course never move anywhere at

all, but are really little cottages with wheels attached. Those that move have one great advantage which does not often apply to boats: you take them home between tours, and can look after them outside your own door without paying a penny for mooring.

Churches and cathedrals

All over the waterways the spires and towers of churches are landmarks. Often you can use them in conjunction with Ordnance Survey maps to discover where you are. And always, as I think ahead on a waterway—or just think of it in memory at other times—a procession of churches seems to sprinkle the scene, outmanoeuvred only now and again by a procession of cooling towers.

There's Braunston spire, of course, to be seen from three different directions, and especially outstanding as you approach from Napton. There's stubby Weston-on-Trent church (the one near Derby), which stands lonely after you think you've passed the village. There are several down the Great Ouse, and a line of sentry churches dotted in the foothill villages all the way down the Nene. There is a peaceful church at Stoak (or Stoke), a few yards from the Wirral Canal short of the chaos of Ellesmere Port, and a pleasant one near to the pubs which flank the narrow channel of the Middle Level at Whittlesey. And Tardebigge's pencil-thin spire is framed in the tunnel exit as you emerge, and stays behind you as you begin to drop down the 58 locks.

The visual memories come quickly now, once I've started. There's Marnham, lonely by the Trent, but looking cowed by the great power station. Stratford's tall spire looks over the landscaped lock marking the mighty Upper Avon achievement, and Alveston further upriver greets those who remember this extra length of navigable Avon. Warwick's tower stands in sight from many of the top locks of Hatton, until it eventually sinks out of view as the boat gets lower. Tamworth tower, unhappily, has been swamped by huge high-rise flats as you

Church: Braunston

come round by Fazeley junction, but Brewood, up the Shroppie, stands across the fields for some time before you reach the village bridge.

There are many more churches, but in particular I find interesting the number of cathedrals which stand near waterways. The Severn, for example, offers two, with Worcester dominating quite a long stretch of your passage by the city, but Gloucester is rather more hidden, and only really in view as you come down the narrow link on the way to welcoming Gloucester lock.

Peterborough cathedral, though squat, is seen clearly across the grass as you cruise by the fine moorings there, but the most striking view comes on leaving Middle Level under the rail bridge, which obligingly frames the cathedral. Ely stands high in the Fens, and can be seen in distant glimpses before you moor under its shadow along the city's pleasant Ouse-side walk.

Cathedral: Peterborough

Lincoln stands even higher, though further from the water. You get a first look at it as you pass the lonely *Pyewipe* inn on the Fossdyke, and it continues to overlook you at the visitors' moorings in Brayford pool, and to peer through a tangle of pylons and cables as you leave the power station on your way down the Witham. It stays in sight almost until Boston Stump (on a church, of course) takes over in the other direction.

York Minster is rather hidden from boats on the Yorkshire Ouse, and on the Leeds & Liverpool Canal you have to be quick to get a glimpse of Blackburn's cathedral somewhat below you after climbing the locks.

Lichfield's three spires, though, are the most elusive, for since the Wyrley & Essington ceased to take boats near to the city we now have to be content with tempting distant views of this fine cathedral through the trees. You can see it after you have struggled through Fradley and entered the long lonely woods

above Woodend lock, but you have to be quick to spot it through the gaps. If you turn down the Coventry instead, you can occasionally see the spires across the relics of the old airfield. In a curious way, these fleeting Lichfield views stay more in the memory than the many churches and cathedrals that stand almost on waterway banks.

Coal

Our canals were built on coal, for one of their chief reasons for existence was the transport of coal from mines to factories and towns. If you spin your propeller fast enough in the Birmingham & Fazeley Canal generations of coal-dust will rise murkily from its bed. And even now, along the Aire & Calder, coal comes out of the ground straight into compartment boats or barges, and up the canal to be gobbled immediately by power stations. (See PUSH-TUGS.)

Coal is an ideal traffic for waterways. It is heavy and a boat is by far the cheapest way of carrying it. There is no great hurry

Coal: Ferrybridge

to get it to its destination, where it may be piled up for months before use; as anyone following a juggernaut load of it nowadays on the roads will agree, it is a confounded nuisance to everybody when carried this way.

So the canals of Britain used to thrive on load after load of coal. Even in 1905 the little Macclesfield's 123,000 tons of freight was mostly coal, though only our broader canals in Yorkshire still carry any large trade now. The fact that the rest have not been modernised to continue transporting it has no doubt helped to put the price where it is.

Recent coal traffic in narrow boats—as distinct from barges and compartment-trains—is an an interesting story. Until only a few years ago there was still a regular trade from the Midlands to factories on the southern Grand Union, with Blue Line and Willow Wren narrow boats a familiar sight. Gradually the traffic fell away, and eventually petered out, with a few individual enthusiasts from the Ashby Canal taking the final loads.

37

Coaster: Purton

Despite the ending of contracts, however, several boats still go up the Ashby, fill up with coal from lorries at Gopsall Wharf, and travel all over the waterway system selling it in polythene bags to anyone who cares to come down to the towpath and fetch it.

These energetic boats are at the same time a sad and a stimulating sight. They are all that remains on the narrow canals of the once-mighty traffic. But they also reflect the initiative and enthusiasm still engendered by canals.

Coasters

Among the surprises—and possibly alarms—of some inland waterways are the occasional appearances of sea-going vessels.

The most likely and most startling place to see one is on the Gloucester-Sharpness Ship Canal. A coaster here is startling because it seems far too big for the waterway. And there certainly does not seem to be room for you as well.

In fact it all works out very nicely, except at the bridges which move out of the way for boats, but many of the coasters will only just squeeze between their piers. Elsewhere ships move so slowly that, despite their seemingly monstrous size, you can pass without difficulty. In fact I have actually overtaken one, waved on by a crew member, though the thought did cross my mind that he might not have contacted the helmsman first.

You meet other coasters on the wider waters of the Weaver, and I remember a remarkable trip down in the Anderton Lift, during which a coaster below us turned itself round in a width of river which did not give it more than a yard or two to spare. It was an interesting lesson in manoeuvring, as we slowly sank to its level in our own full tank of water.

There is the occasional coaster below Gainsborough bridge on the Trent, and of course up the Yorkshire Ouse. But the biggest ocean-going ships on inland waterways are on the Manchester Ship Canal. Few people cruise there with pleasure boats, however, since the rules and regulations are so off-putting that they effectively bar most of us from visiting it.

Cranes

Among old canal relics fighting against developers, destroyers, hooligans, and even waterway authorities are quite a few waterside cranes. You come across them here and there in various stages of preservation or decay, or, as at Sawbridge-worth and on upper Peak Forest, merely as stubs sticking out of the ground.

Braunston has preserved a beauty which I believe is still used, and another at Cheddleton spent years looking wistfully for boats up the Caldon, until BW and wise local authorities made it possible for them to use this beautiful canal again. The pleasant boatyard at Bumblehole on the BCN guards an

unusually-shaped model, and along the Bridgewater there are several cranes standing by to lift the heavy stop-planks needed to span the wide gaps at its bridges.

It is always a bit risky naming things of this kind, for they are liable to vanish as soon as you turn your back. Is that crane still at Lower Heyford, for example? And has anybody backed a car into the one on the wharf at Ellesmere, or moved others elsewhere to build office blocks even as I type this?

They are fascinating gadgets from a past age and it may well be worth making a register of them before they thin out any more.

Cratches

If you are lucky enough to see a commercial narrow boat coming towards you on a narrow canal, the first thing likely to

catch your eye is the cratch, especially if it is gaily-decorated. This is the triangular front board, standing above deck level a little way back from the bows.

The cratch marks the front of the cargo space, and acts as the front support of the planks which usually run along the top of these boats. The gang-planks stretch from the cratch at the front over a number of stands, and finish up—possibly on a downward slope—to rest on a block on the front of the stern cabin. They act as a walkway, and also may serve to support any 'cloths' which need to be used to protect cargoes. When a perishable cargo is fully covered by sidecloths and topcloths, the whole boat looks like a long tent, with the cratch outlining its shape at the front.

There may be a hollow framework of struts a few feet behind the cratch, called the 'false cratch', and the space between the

Cutting: North Oxford Canal

two is usually covered by tarpaulins. Enthusiasts will tell you the different proportions and shapes of cratches from different builders, and also point out that some cratches lean forward, while others may be covered by a canvas framework stuffed with straw or hay, and called a 'bulk'. Nowadays the cratch sometimes acts as a backboard for the tunnel headlamp. Some cratches also can be removed if the cargo is heavy, not perishable, and low in the boat.

Like most of the fascinating components of narrow boats, cratches have been taken over by keen pleasure-boaters, and can often be seen in full rose-and-castle majesty, standing up in front of a converted narrow boat.

Cuttings and embankments

Brindley used to amble miles round a contour to keep his canals on the level, as users of the southern Oxford can well testify. Later canal-diggers, like today's motorway-makers, took straighter routes, moving mounds out of their way and filling up valleys with the same soil.

When you cruise along such canals today their straighter course may be less interesting than the meanderings of earlier canals, but occasionally they make up for it by striking cuttings and lofty embankments.

Even the Gloucester-Sharpness Ship Canal has a wide rocky cutting, the Staffs & Worcs has some gentle sandstone-lined cuttings with an alarming overhanging rock at Austcliff, there's a gloomy one at Tring where the Grand Union reaches its Chiltern summit, the Caledonian has its grim rocky cuttings, and even the BCN acquired a fine one in the end, which has only recently been ruined by road works. But the most startling canal of all for cuttings and embankments is the Shropshire Union main line.

This is the Birmingham & Liverpool Junction from Autherley to Nantwich, the last main canal of the canal age, followed only, much later, by the Manchester Ship Canal and the New Junction. It was built like a railway, as straight as possible from A to B, and so there are great steep-sided cuttings filled with almost tropical growth, and high-striding embankments with tremendous views across to Wales. Both cuttings and embankments have given trouble. Indeed, some of the embankments refused to consolidate, and held up the original opening of the canal. And to this day the banks of the cuttings tend to slide in after rain, or trees crash across and block the canal.

Cruising through a Shroppie cutting can be an eerie experience, with the world as effectively cut out as by any tunnel, and with massive well-protected primroses growing in spring. The channel is sometimes so narrow that it is difficult to pass another boat. But on the embankments, cruising freely on the soil from the cuttings, you seem to be sailing in the sky, with tree-tops and the occasional roof below, and at one place even the chimneys of a pub.

43

Among these remarkable contrasts of scenery, it is a pity that one of the finest cuttings should have been given the unhappy name of Grub Street.

The Macclesfield, too, is a 'cut-and-fill' canal—influenced by the same planner, Telford. It strides along part-way up the hillsides, with views over the Cheshire plain. It does not have the Shroppie's cuttings, but there are some mighty embankments across valleys, which add even more to the views to the west.

Dates

You find them all over the waterways, wherever men built things—on lock walls, balance-beams, paddle-gear, bridges, lock-houses, piling, tunnels, mileposts and notices, and of course also on carefully-maintained old boats. But somehow most of the dates that you see are those of the last-century, and in recent years people seem to have become more reluctant to put dates proudly on whatever they make or build.

So it will be for example 1896 that you see raised in metal on ground paddles (still doing their work after all this time), 1828 in the lock-shoulder below Beeston Iron lock in Cheshire, 1893 over the portal of Standedge tunnel on the closed Huddersfield Narrow, 1861 on No 15 lock of the Wolverhampton flight, 1856 (I think) carved on weatherbeaten stone on a bridge at Gringley Carr on the Chesterfield, and 1854 engraved on Offord lock on the Great Ouse. The only early twentieth-century dates that I recall with any vividness are all those optimistic years cut in the thirties on the concrete piling at the side of the Grand Union in Warwickshire, where in bold lettering the long-silted depths of dredge are also recorded.

Two examples of quite recent dates come to mind. A small plaque at Brighouse gives thanks for the beautifying of the Calder & Hebble surroundings by the local council in 1974—a happy touch. And on a more exciting scale are those beautifully-done notices beside the new locks on the upper Avon. As worthy successors to the brave dates of the nineteenth century, confident twentieth-century dates have appeared. Strongly made in raised metal letters, may they resist twentieth-century vandals and set the fashion again. For the present fine waterway restorations surely deserve permanently-recorded dates that the people of the next century can look at as they cruise.

Detergent

This may seem a curious waterway subject, but all too often it is a waterway sight. In places as far apart as the Aire & Calder near Castleford, the Staffs & Worcs near Wolverhampton and the Nene near Wellingborough great frothy white mounds of the stuff float on the water, with the wind whipping large helpings about like some maniacal candy-floss football game.

The odd thing is that you might meet a mass of detergent on a certain length of waterway at one time, but find no sign of any a few weeks later—though the three places named above are, I believe, regular detergent-topped stretches. But I once saw some

45

blowing about around Whilton bottom lock on the Grand Union, though I've never seen any there before or since.

The powers-that-be, when tackled, will often deny any responsibility for the mess, or at most will say that it is a harmless product of hygienically-treated sewage. But the froth has undoubtedly been a menace in the past, and brought about the use of less frothy detergents. As to the 'harmless' output from sewage works, waterway-users are cynical. You need only cruise on waterways for a few days to see not only large numbers of sewage works alongside you, but also the curious and smelly 'hygienic' liquid that comes from some of them.

The detergent part of it piles up especially at locks, where the disturbances of the water boil up the froth afresh. Sometimes it climbs up the hull of your boat to deck or even window-level, and there is no way of getting rid of it except with a hosepipe, buckets of water or a mop. You may think that it looks whiter than white, and will leave your boat like a new pin. But not a bit of it. If you don't wash if off quickly you find that it eventually dries and leaves nasty little specks of a tarry substance all over your gleaming paintwork.

When you see the froth stirred up again and again as you open lock paddles, alarming thoughts cross your mind. Is this really some terrible attack from outer space? Is it possible that the frothing habit will last for ever, so that the stuff will make its way down our rivers to the sea, until all the oceans of the world are covered by three feet of snowy-white candy-floss?

Diamond-shaped locks

I live in awe of technically minded waterway enthusiasts, and I'm waiting for one of them to tell me why some locks are more or less diamond-shaped. Well, they cannot be exact diamonds, because they can hardly come to points at their ends. But here and there you come across a lock which does not have the useful parallel sides that your boat would prefer, but whose sides consist of walls at various angles.

There's one at Wyre Piddle on the Warwickshire Avon, and

Diamond lock: Wyre Piddle

a very different one not far below at Pershore. I believe some of the vanished old locks on the Upper Avon used to be this shape, and there are two well-known diamond locks on the Oxford Canal. Each of the latter—at Aynho and Shipton—is just below a stretch where the River Cherwell has joined the canal, leaving again above the diamond lock.

This may be a clue to the shape, since each of these Oxford locks lowers boats only a short distance. But presumably the extra width allows the lock to hold much more water, despite its shallow drop, than it would if it were normal width. It can thus keep on passing an ordinary lock-quantity of water down the canal to the other locks, although it is not as deep. Or maybe I've got it all wrong.

The Pershore lock is a mystery, though, for there is nothing shallow about this one. It is one of the deepest and most awkward on the river. And although the greater part of it is 'diamond-shaped', the lowest level has a sort of normal shape in the middle. So if your boat has a deep draught, it can in some circumstances sit on the ledge which sticks out from the walls to form the centre chamber. Slanting ladders on one side, and posts on the other act as guides to drop the boat into the non-diamond centre part when going downstream.

These odd-shaped locks can be awkward for boats in any case, for it is much easier to drive into a lock and lie alongside a perfectly straight side than to have to fiddle about catching on walls at angles. There are locks, too, whose walls are slightly curved, and I believe there are the remains of circular locks somewhere in England. There is certainly one circular lock in France which has three different entrances.

Dog-in-a-Doublet

This ought to be among my 'names' listed elsewhere, but not just for its odd name does it deserve a mention. It is in fact a remarkable lock, named after a nearby lonely pub, at the end of the non-tidal section of the River Nene. It is thus the turn-round point for most inland boats, though in fact many do not bother to go this far. I cannot blame them, for after the fine moorings at Peterborough the remaining 5 miles to the tidal lock are pretty desolate.

From the bend where the route to Stanground and the Middle Level leaves on the right, the river continues in a series of straight stretches linked by a few kinks. Hardly anything is to be seen on the banks, except a small road alongside, and lacking landmarks, the trip to Dog-in-a-Doublet seems endless. Moreover, there is nothing much but the pub and the lock when you get there, but it is, nevertheless, an interesting boundary-point on inland waterways.

There is a useful place to tie up if no-one is waiting for the lock, and you can examine the great network of girders which makes up the barrage and the supports for the guillotine gates of the lock, towering up to dominate the lock-keeper's bungalow. Then if it is opening time, perhaps a look at the tidal river below, and a drink before the dull slog back to Peterborough.

Dog-in-a-Doublet

Dogs

People either like dogs or thoroughly disapprove of them. Some people like their own dogs but disapprove of other people's. Regardless of human beings, however, most dogs like waterways, and there really ought to be a dogs' IWA. They like cruising on boats, running across lock-gates, lock-wheeling up towpaths, and even falling in.

Other people's dogs are a nuisance if they have been on your hired boat the week before you, for a surprising number of them seem to sleep on their owner's bed. Your own dog is a nuisance in wet weather, he brings half the towpath back aboard every time he arrives—you are doing just the same yourself.

49

Most cruises are punctuated by regular encounters with dogs on the banks barking their heads off as you go by. Some are alsatians guarding scrapyards—a common feature of canals in particular; others are farm dogs which think they own the whole countryside. One, near Hillmorton, used to go quite hysterical every time a boat passed, and could hardly have had much energy left for farming in summer. An alsatian on the Worcester & Birmingham seemed to be fascinated by a boat's wash, and used to trot frantically up and down peering at it until it subsided. And a dog once followed me for miles along the Lancaster from Bridge 131, barking and having a drink, until his territory expired at the M6.

Clever as they are at crossing lock-gates, dogs can still fall in. And though they will always swim even if they have never been in the water before, they cannot get out of an empty lock with closed gates. This was once given to me as the reason why the northern Stratford locks are supposed to be left empty with open gates—though I never managed to have it confirmed officially. Nor can dogs climb out of well-piled pounds between locks; I've rescued one near the Fishery Inn and another from a pound in the Perry Barr flight. They are never very grateful.

On the whole, however, dogs are very suitable for waterways, unless they happen to be crazy about sheep or cows. And why shouldn't they enjoy canals and rivers? We do.

Dropping things in

Twice I have met people who might be termed beachcombers of the waterways. One was flinging in a small grappling-iron at the head of a lock near Fradley, and the other was dangling a powerful magnet at the foot of one on the Staffs & Worcs. Each was looking for lost windlasses, which with moderate frequency end up on the bottom near locks.

Windlasses are the most unfortunate things for anyone to drop into the water—especially if they have no spare. And it is only too easy to drop one in if it is foolishly left unattended on a spindle, or if it slips as you are turning. It can fall off a balance beam while you open or close a gate, or you can put it down temporarily while dealing with something else, thereby ensuring that you or somebody else kicks it in.

But there are other things besides windlasses which sometimes end up on the waterway bed: tools, for example. If you have an outboard or outdrive engine you may have to attend to it with your head hanging over the back of the boat, and using various spanners, mole-wrenches, screwdrivers or pliers. Inevitably one slips, and plop! It is thus only sensible to attach them to your wrist, if possible with a piece of string.

You may get a more awkward result if you have to remove the propeller. Both the propeller and the various parts which hold it on can easily leave your hands if you catch them on something, or even if you jog your funny-bone. So hold them lovingly and closely, preferably with two hands at a time.

Somewhere near the *Rock of Gibraltar* on the Oxford Canal I once inadvertently cast in a dinner-plate, and no doubt there are many frying-pans, tea-pots and saucepans scattered throughout our waterways where people have just casually swilled them round and made to empty the contents over the side. Then there must be numerous tea-cups, saucers and beer-tankards, thrown off roofs by the wash of passing cowboys. Hats, towels, pullovers and guides to the waterways are often deposited overboard by strong winds, and I gather that outside West Stockwith lock in the Trent there are numerous anchors thrown hastily overboard by people who forgot to attach them to their boats.

One way and another, then, quite apart from the rubbish deliberately put in by large numbers of the public, our waterway beds must yield a remarkable harvest of things dropped in by boaters alone. Some no doubt will prove most mystifying to future archaeologists.

Ducks

Swans are the proudest, most interesting, and sometimes the fiercest of waterway birds, and moorhens are the most common.

But ducks, I think, are the friendliest. They quack away, wagging their beaks and tails, and twiddling their bodies here and there when a boat approaches. They seem to learn at a surprisingly fluffy age that most boaters have bits of stale bread around, just waiting for a duck. Thus Mum and Dad and a flock of balls of fluff are always ready to receive.

The drakes are brightly-coloured, with the females a drabber blotchy brown. Along parts of the Lancaster Canal, for some reason, there seems to be a surplus of drakes, looking rather puzzled at the absence of mates. Or maybe I happened to come across some male convention, away from all the nest-making and egg-laying.

When ducks take to the air they assume a much less lumpy shape. The rather absurd swimmers, begging for scraps, become swift determined arrows though the air, heading unswervingly for a destination known only to themselves.

Dudley tunnel

This is a fascinating tunnel in the Black Country, wrapped with mystery. Since Standedge, Sapperton and Lappal went out of use Dudley has long been proclaimed as the longest tunnel still more or less usable, with its length given as 3172 yd—well, all

right, 2900 metres.

Dudley was not in fact usable for a long time, but recently the locks leading to it have been repaired, dredging has been carried out, and it is now again possible to travel through. But you are not allowed to use an engine (see LEGGING), and many cabin-topped boats are too large for the restricted shape of the tunnel.

Many people have been surprised to discover that the much-vaunted 2900m length does not in fact apply to a continuous tunnel. The journey includes a large basin open to the skies at Castle Mill, where the first long tunnel ends. You cross this open-air area and enter another small tunnel to a smaller basin, before a further tunnel brings you into the open air for the last time. By no stretch of the imagination can the whole thing be referred to as a single tunnel.

The Canal Trust's map shows the main tunnel length as 2904 yd (2655m), which puts it below Blisworth, Netherton and Harecastle in the tunnel league. This is all very sad, and I hope I have not upset the marvellous Trust which made its reopening possible. But that's how it looks to me.

All the same, it really is the most incredible tunnel in the whole waterway system, unless you count the old Worsley

workings. It took seven awkward years to build, and is not only a weird mixture of brickwork, rough rock and caverns, but contains old quarries of its own, with various branches that once had their own tramways. It is far from being the straightforward hole (or three holes?) through a hill that most canal tunnels are.

As an interesting postscript, even the figure of 2900m usually quoted for the total length was queried recently. A work party legged their way through in a 70ft boat and actually measured it. They came out with a total of 3154yd, or 2884m. But even they do not seem to have noticed the sky above them in Castle Mill Basin.

Flags

Flowers are among the special attractions of waterways, and they flourish along the banks even when lack of rain elsewhere has caused them to shrivel and die. They grow in mightier sizes there, too, with their feet always moist and rich silt to feed on. Many common flowers line waterway banks; primroses in spring grow especially lusciously in Shropshire Union cuttings

54

and all along the Brecon. Bluebells carpet woods on the Lancaster, and in later months meadow-sweet marches down to many a water's edge.

But there are some which are specifically waterway flowers, from lilies which float on the surface (on the way to Slough, for example), to the wild forget-me-nots which do far better than in any garden. To my mind, however, the wild iris is the most symbolic waterway flower of them all, and I am surprised that the old canal boats were not decorated with painted irises rather than roses.

The wild iris or flag by the water is yellow, and its life in June is unhappily short. But if you go up the Ashby, for example, you can see these aristocratic flowers marching ahead of you for miles. A few in a vase seem to do no harm to the rest, for like those in the garden their rhizomes go creeping onwards for ever. Keen students of nature tell me that the iris has an unusual one-way system for bees, which prevents the flowers from pollinating themselves.

Floating restaurants

Comparative newcomers to the waterways, restaurants afloat fall into two categories. There are those that move and those that do not—though the latter are always in danger of developing into odd contraptions that no longer could be termed 'boats'. They grow top-heavy superstructures—even two storeys—covered gangplanks and other appendages.

Among the non-moving types I remember the unexpected *Ba Ba Gee* moored in the basin at that far-flung waterway outpost of Glasson, off the Lancaster Canal. There's one on the Severn at Shrewsbury, and the *Barque & Bite* has stood—or floated—near the London Zoo for some years now. Recently two barges have appeared at the top end of the Rochdale Canal locks in Manchester, with a bar in one and a restaurant in the other. I've heard of another on the Yorkshire Ouse, but none in Birmingham yet, though there are plenty of trip-boats loaded with beer and snacks.

The permanently-moored restaurants as boats seem to me to be a bit of a fraud since, to all intents and purposes, you might as well still be on land, especially at night when it is dark outside. The more recent idea of eating a pleasant meal on a moving boat is a more intriguing experience. The earliest example was *Tyseley*, which travelled from Thrupp near Oxford along the Oxford Canal, with diners eating among soft lights as they looked out on the passing countryside. But *Tyseley*, alas, has gone.

There are two newer ones, though. *The Lace Plate*, with curtains to match its name, first cruised from Braunston through lonely countryside, but along a waterway often busy with boats. *Windlass* is based at Clifton near Rugby, and its journey includes the short Newbold tunnel as well as both the Rugby outskirts and some trees and empty fields.

These boats offer freshly-cooked food, though without such a wide choice as ashore, but with imaginative and varying menus. They have bars on board and a refreshingly limited number of diners. It is to be hoped that more such boats will appear, for it is a relaxing change for anyone looking for a pleasant meal out.

Don't, by the way, confuse floating restaurants with the large numbers of trip-boats now to be found. They need to be approached with care for they range from the clean and well-kept to others where you will find last night's beer-party dregs still swimming everywhere.

Galton tunnel

Of all the tunnels on the canals, this is the most intriguing. First, it is the newest, having appeared only in 1974, and second, it is not really a tunnel at all in the sense of a hole dug through a hill for a waterway; for the tunnel was put there first and the hill then placed on top of it.

You will find it in the historic BCN cutting where Telford lowered the Wolverhampton route to get rid of the inconvenient locks that held boats up around Smethwick. Until 1974 the cutting swept majestic and open, deep below the Black

Country roar, and with rich blackberry bushes on its slopes. But someone has now dropped a huge concrete pipe into the canal at one point, and covered it with a vast hill of dirt. On top runs a new road and the pipe, complete with towpath and railings, has become British Waterways' newest tunnel, 123yd (or 112m) long.

The birth of Galton may have been intriguing, but it is not too popular with canal enthusiasts. It has not only ruined the majesty of the striking cutting, but has almost blocked the view of the fine Galton Bridge which sweeps its tracery high above from one side to the other. Now, as you come out of the pipe, you must crick your neck to look quickly up to the bridge before another bridge hides it again.

Some years ago a motorway on stilts spoilt the nearby sight of the Stewart (or Steward) Aqueduct taking the Old Main Line over the New Line. Now Galton Bridge's splendour has been swamped. Ah well, there are still the blackberries in August.

Gasworks

The interesting thing about Gas Street Basin in Birmingham—now almost as impassable because of trip-boats as when there was a physical bar across the canal—is that no gasworks seem to be visible there. But plenty of other places along the waterways make up for this. Indeed, I have often taken photographs of an interesting canal scene, only to discover that a couple of gasometers have grown to dominate the picture during development.

Sometimes these monsters add a sort of striking beauty to the view, rather as the cooling towers of electricity power stations bring lengths of the Trent and the BCN to life. Heading down the Canal into Coventry, for example, you meet high gasometers on your right and weeping willows on your left, in

58

Glasson

fascinating company. Near Kensal Green, as you approach
Paddington, huge gasometer frames are soon followed by an
equally spectacular overhanging motorway. And in many other
places people seem for some reason to have built their gasworks
near to canals or rivers.

You can understand why electricity power stations are so
often alongside a river, for you can see the steam coming from
the water they have used. And it is also fairly obvious why
canals so often seem to have sewage works on their banks
(though nobody will ever admit to a reason here). But why so
many gasworks as we cruise?

Glasson

The Lancaster Canal is not really counted as a canal by many
canallers. It is difficult for them to get there, as it is not

connected to the rest of the system, and above all there isn't a lock on it from one end of its present 41 miles to the other. Thus anyone from the main waterways who finds himself there on a boat feels something is a bit odd—apart from the luxurious cruisers streaming along in the sunshine with their hoods still up, for all the world like cars on the M6 alongside.

But there is compensation, for a handy little $2\frac{7}{8}$-mile branch leaves near Galgate, and offers a vigorous opportunity for anyone who is lost without locks. In that short distance seven great Leeds-&-Liverpool-type locks help you down the hill to the curious port of Glasson, where coasters come in from the sea. Massive scissor-like sluice-boards on the lock-gates, and some tough ground paddles, will require a fair bit of grunting and pushing to get some of the gates open. And in a fierce cross-wind some heavy boat-handling will be needed as you slog down towards sea-level.

Glasson itself is removed from this world, yet several pubs and cafés (including a floating restaurant) seem to indicate a tourist trade on summer days. At other times it can be a bleak and empty spot, where even the ample moorings in the canal basin can be choppy. There is a swing-bridge and lock into the sea-dock, and the Lune estuary outside. Everyone cruising the Lancaster should lock down to Glasson and back, if only to avoid nodding off at the tiller on the main canal.

Great Ouse river

The Great Ouse area is almost as cut off from the main waterways as are the Norfolk Broads—but not quite. Boats can in fact make a complicated journey from the Grand Union down 17 locks to Northampton, 37 River Nene locks to Peterborough, and then through the Middle Level Drains and eventually on a short tidal dash to Denver Sluice. But this is too involved, and for most people takes too long, so the Great Ouse and its tributaries retain a distinctly different character from other waterways.

Until a few years ago boats paid no fees to cruise here, but

Great Ouse: Godmanchester

now, reasonably, they need licences, and this provides at least some money towards making the navigation easier. The locks do much flood control, obviously, and like those of the Nene almost all have guillotines at one end—sometimes the top, sometimes the bottom. Few locks look alike, and two—at Earith and Roxton—are brand new, the former replacing an ancient structure. Soon there will be other new ones.

Every kind of cruising is available. From Denver you continue the Middle Level pattern of wide waters with high banks making for invisible views. But above Ely you can go up the friendlier and narrowing Cam to Cambridge, or turn to the winding Old West, which is more like a canal than a river. This brings you to the tidal cut-off at Earith where the Ouse sends much water straight to sea. But above Brownshill you are on typical flat, winding river more like the Nene. It is less lonely than the Nene, though, for there are St Ives, Huntingdon and St Neots, as well as several villages, and quite a succession of marinas, some delightfully situated. There are fewer locks, too, than on the Nene, and in fact the atmosphere and the types of boat are more like the superior Thames.

If you want to be lonely, you should turn off the lower reaches into the Wissey, the Little Ouse or the Lark. These tributaries are far less busy, so don't expect the crowded waterside pubs and pricey restaurants that you meet on the upper river.

The Ouse system is rather chromium-plated by most canal boaters' standards, but it is at least the scene of one vigorous piece of restoration. The unnavigable gap below Bedford is well on its way to being reopened; gradually one lock after another is being rebuilt, so that in time Bedford will be reached from the rest of the Great Ouse waters.

Hand-spikes

Most regular waterway users reckon that they've come across every imaginable type of paddle-gear. They have used windlasses with big holes and windlasses with little holes, as well as windlasses with two holes, to turn spindles on cogs or worms which somehow or other lift up or slide coverings away from holes under the water. Sometimes the turning handles are already fixed to the gear, and in the case of guillotines of course they raise the whole gate instead of just a bit of it.

There is one very unusual system, however, which I believe is unique to the Calder & Hebble. Here, many locks have paddle-gear which is worked by means of a hand-spike, and woe betide you if you have not brought one. This instrument is a handy, club-like hunk of hardwood about a yard long, one end forming a 2in by 3in rectangle. This fits into the slots of a small cylinder low down on the ground or gate, which can then be revolved by heaving the hand-spike up and over. Some attached cogs are turned, and bring up the usual type of rack, raising the

sluice-cover way down below.

You have to keep extracting the spike from its slot and placing it in another ready to heave over again. But this does seem the simplest method imaginable of levering up a rack. Occasionally spikes can be found attached to the gear, but don't bank on it. And as you lever away, think what a handy weapon one of these must have made in any boatmen's argument in years gone by.

Headgear

The problem of headgear on inland waterways seems to be solved by different people in different ways. The most surprising hats—to me anyway—are the bus-conductor-cum-naval-officer types with their snow-white tops, shiny peaks, and indeterminate badges. I never knew whether their wearers are in fact former naval officers (or bus conductors?) or whether they wear them as some kind of indication that they are the official captain of the boat they are on. So I do not know whether to salute or to offer my fare.

Another form of headgear, especially popular on narrow boats, is the navy blue or black European-peasant style. This too has a peak, but the rest is a soft undulating shape, obviously well-suited for dropping in the water or for carrying crumpled-up in pockets—or even for tying up with string and using as a football.

There is a vigorous tribe of devotees of the bobble-hat, a knitted woollen skullcap with a large pom-pom, or bobble, on top. Usually they are in two colours, with alternate rings of colour going round the skull. I was intrigued for many years by the bobble on the top, until it was explained that this forms an excellent buffer between the head and the sharp top-edge of the doorway through which canallers in particular often have to move rapidly. Certainly my own skull could have done with a buffering bobble many times. On the Broads there is always a

64

fair sprinkling of Kiss-me-quick headgear, more suitable for fairgrounds—as indeed its wearers often are.

The point about headgear, I would have thought, is surely the purpose it serves. If you regard it as a pure status-symbol, then obviously you will go in for the naval/bus conductor kind. And if—despite being on inland waters—you want to look as if you are a dashing yachtsman, then perhaps the bobble-hat is the thing. But my own idea is that a hat is either (a) to keep off the rain, or (b) to keep off the sun.

To keep off the rain a sou'wester takes some beating, since it sheds the water it receives well clear of the neck instead of down it. But my own biggest problem is keeping off the sun, which peels me rapidly. A bobble-cap is useless for this, and it seems to me that both the naval/bus conductor and the European-peasant types fail in one important respect: they do not shade either the ears or the back of the neck. They keep the forehead from peeling, and perhaps the nose. But those delicate tips of the ears, and that vulnerable back of the neck are still exposed to the wicked sun—if you're that kind, of course. (I know that being fashionable and growing a head of hair like a boat-mop solves these problems, but I have not quite got to that yet).

So I commend the straw hat to you. It looks reasonably neat, it is light, it keeps the sun off you all round, and when it blows off it floats—though the snag is that it does tend to blow off quite often, since the rim forms an excellent parachute. But if you feel a straw hat is rather too sedate or Edwardian, then try one of those floppy bush-hats they sell in camping shops. That, too, shades you all round, stands up to a lot of abuse, and can look dashing in a jungly sort of way. The naval officers won't speak to you, though.

Hooks

The hooks I mean are funny little curved things, only a few inches long, still to be found in the corners of some lock shoulders down the Tardebigge flight. These puzzled me for

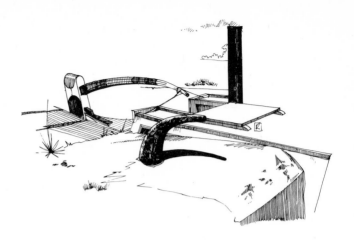

some time until I happened to mention them in public, after which I was inundated by helpful explanations.

It seems that they were used to give purchase to the horses in getting boats moving out of the locks—always a strenuous job. A loop of rope was placed round the hook at the lock corner in front of the boat, the rope was then run back through a pulley on the boat and forward again to the horse. The hook then took half the load when the horse pulled. As the boat passed the hook (which faced away from it) the loop slipped off and the rope ran back until a wood stop fixed to the rope prevented it from running out of the pulley. By this time the boat was happily on its way to the next lock.

Gadgets for this purpose were used in many places on the BCN, too, and I have seen pulley-wheels on the Regent's Canal and elsewhere. Some odd-shaped bollards on the Calder & Hebble look as if they might have been used for the same sort of job, since they curve away from the boat. Indeed, I think the whole business of gadgets at locks is an interesting study. Look, for example, for lock-wall sockets for the use of barge-poles.

Horseway

The journey through the Middle Level Drains is one of

66

contrasts. Most of the cruising consists of broad deep waters, almost like some of the smaller Dutch canals. There is nothing much to see even over the high banks, but steering is somnolently easy, with the straight channel running away in front of you for miles. But getting in and out of this near-100-mile network is less relaxing. The three links with the outside world involve struggles with shallow routes and strange locks.

The lock at Horseway is on one of these links. You approach it from inside the Drains either straight along the broad Forty Foot, or down the 9-mile Sixteen Foot, which brings you left into the tail-end of the Forty Foot. Then immediately you are in a different kind of channel. It is narrow and overhung with trees, with reeds and weed growing in it—either new and vigorous or old and dead according to the time of year. You may also even meet dumped rubbish as you move cautiously alongside bushes, and approach the antiquated structure of the

67

Hotel Boat: Bracken

lock—often called a 'sluice' in those parts.

It looks ancient and it is hard work, but laboriously it does its job. The key to the odd paddle-gear is supposed to be locked in a container alongside, but most canallers will have a windlass that fits the spindles. Then gradually the boat will rise from the Drains below sea-level, nearer to the higher waters beyond the next lock at Welches Dam—another curious contraption.

Horseway is a weird and deserted place in this strange open Fenland country. And by the time you have cleared the weed and worked the paddles and the gates, you will have had plenty of opportunity to look around you.

Hotel boats

Not everyone is able or inclined to handle a boat on waterways. Thus recent years have seen a flock of 'cruising hotels' or 'hotel boats' roaming the system.

In fact—surprising to many—the first pair of such boats

68

appeared at the Market Harborough IWA Rally in 1950. Soon afterwards two were based at Penkridge, and in 1953 Michael Streat—waterway pioneer in many things—started regular hotel boat cruises. But it is only in the last few years that hotel boating has really grown.

Almost all these boats are on canals, and normally a pair of 70ft long and 7ft wide boats work together, one towing the other. There are variations though. *Tranquil Rose* travels on her own but is roomier in width, at 12ft 6in. She is unable to tackle the narrow canals, but cruises the wide-lock area of the eastern Trent & Mersey, the Trent, the Fossdyke and the Soar. *Bracken* also cruises on her own and is only 62ft by 7ft, so she can travel waterways such as the Leeds & Liverpool with shorter locks. She also takes only five passengers. In contrast another 'hotel' consists of three 70ft boats in a group—a formidable collection.

Inland Waterway Holiday Cruises, of Preston Brook near Warrington, have three pairs of boats in the traditional style, with the 'motor' towing the 'butty', and with the traditional roses and castles, brasswork and white ropes. This firm's *Jupiter* and *Saturn*, *Mabel* and *Forget-me-not*, and now *Snipe* and *Taurus*, are well-known canal travellers.

The word 'hotel' may be misleading without a little thought, for obviously on a 7ft-wide boat you can't expect a large hotel room. Cabins are bound to be small, and facilities rather limited. But there is always a saloon and a dining room, small open-air areas, and quite small numbers of guests. The pace of travel is such that passengers can stroll along the towpath ahead of the boat. A couple of 70ft boats usually carry 12 passengers between them.

Some hotel boats—such as two on the Brecon—have been built especially for their job, and others have been skilfully converted from boats with fascinating trading histories. *Saturn*, for example, was built of oak and elm in 1906, and once carried cheese from Shropshire and Cheshire to Manchester. *Mallard* and *Dabchick*, working from Braunston, used to carry a variety of cargoes up the Grand Union Canal.

Historical or no, these hotel boats now offer a unique

waterway experience to anyone unfamiliar with canals in particular, and prepared to accept limited quarters (but often magnificent food). And when you book, ask for a cabin in the butty. This is the one without an engine, and as you travel you can hear only the ripple of water past the hull.

Inland Waterways Association

Anybody—boater or not—who is seriously interested in inland waterways joins the IWA. One day somebody will write its stirring history, for there is no doubt at all that without the Association very many more miles of our waterways would have become derelict, and many miles of canals and rivers now in use would never have been restored.

Yet whoever writes the IWA's history will need to tread a delicate path, for any group of indignant people is bound to find some of its indignation flying around internally at times. Thus there have been family conflicts now and again, both open and politely veiled. There have been sorrowful resignations, and occasional accusations and counter-accusations, and sometimes mystification among common-or-garden members as to what it's all about.

Apart from a certain amount of friendly banter over non-traditional-shaped boats, the chief IWA internal differences seem to have been over attitudes to authority. In the early days waterway authorities were roundly abused much of the time, until it was realised that constantly putting people's backs up is not really the best way of persuading them to do anything. So gradually the Association has come to admit that the British Waterways Board, especially, actually exists, and may even be approached at times by means of normal rational argument. A few disgusted members may have gone off in a huff at the thought, but a surprising amount has been achieved by dialogue, when one considers how starved the Board is of money.

Yet the IWA is far from being a body of complacent yes-men now. Its Inland Shipping Group campaigns as vigorously—and in civilised fashion—as the Association has ever campaigned. All over the country, branches agitate as well as liaise along local waterways, and in particular with local authorities, who are now playing an unheard-of part in restorations and clean-ups.

Members labour strongly in many ways, from shovelling mud to writing letters, from humping old bedsteads out of canals to canvassing MPs, from organising rallies to collecting old newspapers. And the sum total is a surprisingly live waterway system, despite the still-chronic lack of government funds for maintenance.

The IWA attracts a wide variety of people, and it is not surprising that they are sometimes at odds with each other over the complex matter of inland waterways—whether it is about the direction of the Association's aims, or its methods of carrying them out. But its complaining nostalgic few are quite wrong in implying that it is now too respectable and complacent and conforming. It is still kicking strongly, and it has achieved far more than if it had merely acted like a bad-tempered little boy who knows only rude words.

It is possible to agitate and even be aggressive without having to be uselessly objectionable. And this is more likely to make a positive impact on people. The IWA nowadays seems to be achieving this in no uncertain fashion.

Keadby

This place—which as a lad I used to know as 'Kidby'—is a well-known waterway landmark on the Trent, at the limit of the downriver navigation for most inland boats. The river can be tricky enough as far down as Keadby, but only those with experience and the right boat should go further, for Trent Falls and the lower Ouse are no place for anyone else.

There is a high lock gate on your left just below Keadby Bridge, and this is where inland craft should climb up to the Sheffield & South Yorkshire Navigation (or Stainforth & Keadby Canal). But it is no good coming down the river at the

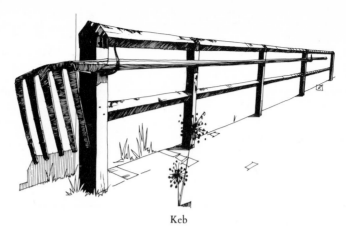

Keb

wrong time. You would battle against the tide, meet the eagre (or aegir, or aegre), go aground—you name it, the Trent supplies it—and you might well end up pottering about unable to get into Keadby lock for hours. Ask at Cromwell lock, ring up the Keadby lock-keeper, then roll down the 43½ tidal miles to turn into the current at Keadby and go into the lock gates. But it is a long way up to catch the keeper's eye.

Up there in the canal above the river you are in a quieter world. There is a strange lost village around you, and a curious sliding railway bridge ahead on the long flat ride towards Sheffield. And there are fish and chips and three pubs if you moor at Keadby for the night.

Kebs

I often have the odd feeling that waterways are quite divorced from the rest of the world. Physically they seem to be so as you cruise or walk along them, even in the heart of cities, and some of the language used about waterways seems never to have penetrated outside their banks.

You will not even find in an ordinary dictionary, the waterway uses of such words as 'paddle', 'windlass', 'stank', 'cratch', 'nip', 'staircase', 'butty', or even 'pound', nor the waterway meanings of the verbs 'to wind', 'to leg', and 'to

72

lock'. You will not find at all the word 'gongoozler', or the well-known Thames term, 'rimer'. And surprisingly you will search in vain for 'keb'.

I really set out merely to discuss kebs, but was sidetracked into seeing what the dictionary said about them, and it does not say anything at all. It struck me as remarkable that such a long-established waterway word, together with so many even more common ones, should not yet have come to the notice of dictionary-compilers. Yet all the words mentioned above, for example, were listed and defined in Rudolph de Salis's *Bradshaw's Canals and Navigable Rivers*, published in 1904, so they must have been in use long before then, and most are used regularly without thought by most people around waterways today.

However, let us return to the keb—a word perhaps not quite so common as some of the others. According to de Salis, it is 'an iron rake used for fishing up coal or other articles from the bottom of a canal'; to which Edwards, in his modern *Inland Waterways of Great Britain*, rather quaintly adds: 'Boatmen may often be seen fishing for coal in this way at coal wharves'. Well, I have not come across this pastime very often, but I have seen plenty of kebs, and any canal user must have met them. They are the long-handled things, with prongs at right angles to the handle, often found in a rack alongside a lock—though I must admit that many lock-keepers seem to call them merely 'rakes' nowadays.

I first met one as a boy, when it was being used to drag weed out of the Chesterfield Canal; and trying to give a hand I pulled myself in instead of the weed out. Since then I have often seen kebs used for fishing around lock-gates for bricks, oil-drums, timber, branches, tyres, and any other floating or sunken objects. They do not seem to be as common as they once were, but they are an interesting example of a simple tool serving a useful purpose. I've no doubt that in their time they have played many parts, from hooking out lost windlasses to yanking out fallen-in people.

Leaves

Leaves play several parts in a waterway user's life. Their colours in spring, for example, take the breath away. They seem more vivid and varied along lush waterway banks than anywhere else. There seems to be a certain point in the year—usually in May—when the range of leaf-colours appears to outdo the rainbow. You can hardly believe that they will all be easing off to a few dullish shades of green before long.

At the other end of the year, though, after the mellow autumn colours, those same leaves can make themselves a rather curious kind of nuisance. On such tree-lined canals as the southern Staffs & Worcs they can lie so thickly on the water that your propeller attracts great balls of them. This alters its effect, and stops it from from doing its job properly. It does not matter much so long as you potter along, but it can be alarming when you go into reverse and try to stop. During one memorable autumn day several times I bumped into lock-shoulders because the leaves were sucked to my propeller and prevented it from stopping me. This was the first time I had come across the effect of floating leaves. There is always something new to learn on the water, so beware of thick carpets of floating leaves.

There are leaves under the water, too, during much of the summer—ones that grow there. On such rivers as the Nene, and I recall on the Ashby Canal and the Slough Arm, you find an underwater weed with cabbage-like leaves and stems as tough as rope which wind lovingly round your prop. Various lesser leaves can also cause trouble, but you would think the tiny-leaved duckweed would be no bother. Try the Rufford Branch of the Leeds & Liverpool, then. I have seen duckweed there growing so thickly that the wind piled it up into mounds. On one bend I was brought to a stop by a sheer mass of it across the channel. On such waters—and even where there is much less of it—the stuff seems to get everywhere, and you are cleaning the minute flecks of green from both inside and outside the boat for days afterwards.

Arrow-shaped leaves wave about on some water-weeds, and the tall leaves of various reeds and rushes bow down as you approach, and rise up again laughing after you have passed by.

Although there is nothing more wonderful than the fresh spring leaves along a cruise, waterways also have an especial appeal when there are no leaves on the trees at all. Every tree-lined journey produces new views not visible in summer. And canals which in the main cruising season are just tunnels through overhanging trees suddenly show you distant fields and hills and villages which you did not know existed.

Legging

This curious activity is regarded by most people as a thing of the past, which disappeared when canal boats were motorised. But in one place at least it still goes on, the newly-reopened Dudley tunnel (qv).

Legging was the method used to propel boats through tunnels which had no towpath for a horse. He went off over the top, and leggers lay on boards on the boat and walked along the tunnel sides. In narrow tunnels the boards could lie across the boat, but when a narrow boat went through a broad tunnel such as those on the Grand Union, the legging-boards had to be extended outwards from the boat sides so that the leggers' feet could reach the tunnel walls. This must have been not only a strenuous but also precarious occupation, since a fall into the water in a pitch-black tunnel would make rescue very difficult.

Nowadays occasional enthusiasts try legging for fun (there was once a 'sponsored leg' through Blisworth tunnel for charity), and occasionally a breakdown in a tunnel may lead to some unexpected legging and poling on the roof. But the legging necessary in Dudley tunnel is due to the fact that boats are not allowed to use their engines because of ventilation problems. Thus if your boat will fit the tunnel (and not all boats will) you can try to emulate Dudley Canal Trust experts and leg it through—but don't forget to take your boards to lie on. Since Dudley is only the width of a narrow boat, however, you

Lime juice

can always remain standing and push yourself through with
your hands.

Lime juice

This unusual liquid has a special place of honour in waterway
history. As I write it remains the only regular narrow boat
cargo on the Grand Union Canal. Coal travels sporadically up
and down, but after the regular coal traffic south from the
midlands ceased, the carriage of lime juice from Brentford to
Rose's at Boxmoor was all that kept the historic narrow boat
traffic flag regularly flying.

Things can change quickly. It may itself have ceased before
these words are in print. I hope not. On the other hand, new
traffic may have been started by vigorous enthusiasts. But
Banbury and *Buxton* will have an honoured place for carrying
heavy drums from Brentford docks, up the sweeping Hanwell
Flight, and eventually on to the quayside under the tall blocks
of Hemel Hempstead. The ghosts of thousands of boatmen,
running loaded narrow-boats, must travel with this pair.

76

Lincoln

Lincoln sits high in a remarkable position, even more striking than Ely, with almost all the land in sight as flat as a pancake. From a waterways point of view you approach it from the Trent on the Fossdyke, with its broad, straight stretches, and you leave it again along the Witham, with its even broader, straighter stretches. And Lincoln is there as a welcome calling place in the broadness, straightness and flatness.

You can see Lincoln miles before you get there, and see it behind you until Boston Stump begins to loom ahead. The most interesting sight of it is beyond the isolated Pyewipe inn, standing on the Fossdyke bank. Then you begin to pass the racecourse, moored boats and lift-bridges before coming into wide Brayford Pool almost in the heart of the city.

Recent water festivals have begun to put Lincoln on the waterway map, and it is to be hoped that Brayford will develop into a fine place instead of the rather shallow and tatty-looking area that it used to be. You keep to the left as you pass through it, and visitors' moorings are marked there—though not recommended for peace and quiet. The Witham comes in surreptitiously at the far right-hand corner, and as you leave Brayford you are in fact now on the river.

There used to be a cantankerous movable bridge here which irritated both boaters and motorists, but great areas of concrete have now replaced it. You then pass an interesting length which includes Marks & Spencers on one wide and Woolworths on the other, with the famous Glory Hole, or High Bridge, with its black-and-white buildings straddling over you. There will be masses of swans, too, and you can almost tie up to shops between two noisy car parks.

As far as noise is concerned, it is perhaps as well to carry on, past where the grain traffic came until recently, and where old waterway pubs recently stood. At the guillotine-gated Stamp End lock, with its rolling footbridge, there is a lock-keeper to help you, and a water-tap lurking on the left above the lock. Beyond the lock is a deceptive bridge which looks easily clearable but probably isn't. It does not look as if it will move,

Lock cabin

either, but when you have unearthed the bridge-keeper from his hideout on the right, you find that he can in fact raise it inch by inch, staying horizontal though, until you can pass under it.

I have been so busy getting us through Lincoln I have omitted to mention that all the time the cathedral is standing high above, looking down on the whole business. And at some time or other you should clamber up the hill to it. You will be puffing by the time you reach the top, but it is downhill back again.

As you make off down the seemingly endless Witham towards its sugar-beet factory, you pass an obstrusive power station, but the cathedral keeps on looking at you through the tangle of pylons.

Lock cabins

Locks used to have lock houses with lock-keepers—important

chaps who worked long hours to keep the commerce moving on waterways everywhere. Gradually their numbers have thinned out especially on canals, where you can cruise for a week and never come across a lock-keeper. Most of their houses have emptied, been vandalised, and eventually ended up as overgrown heaps of bricks with wild lilac and roses where gardens once flourished. More fortunate houses have been acquired by waterway enthusiasts and lovingly restored.

Lock-keepers do in fact still exist, even on canals. But usually they look after vast numbers of locks and double up with other jobs too. Some complicated flights of locks continue to have their own keepers, perhaps rechristened Water Controllers, and sometimes you meet groups of locks neatly mown and maintained beyond the call of duty.

On most rivers and some commercial canals there is still a keeper at each lock, reigning over its operation. The Thames, the Trent, the Severn, the Weaver (but not, curiously, the Nene) have keepers at every lock, and every Lee and Stort lock has a lock house—though I have seen few keepers there. Many of these locks, as also those on the Yorkshire navigations such as the Aire & Calder, have little cabins where the keepers perch, especially if the locks are worked electrically.

They sit in these well-windowed eyries, waiting for you to approach. Perhaps, on less busy routes, you see them crossing purposefully from their houses at the sound of your siren. Then they press their buttons and operate traffic-lights for you, and thus remotely pass you through without any human contact.

This is the snag about these control-cabins. The operator is no longer a friendly human to chat to as the water-level changes. He is a robot, seen only from a distance—and indeed, not seen at all for most of the time when you lurk in some locks, as on the Trent. And when you have left, you rub your eyes and wonder if there really was ever anybody there at all.

Yet these cabin-dwellers are in fact friendly human beings, as you find if you ever have need to swarm ashore. Some on the Severn can even lean out of their windows and chat with you as you sink or rise. One of the things to surprise you is that they

79

knew all about you before you arrived. They not only seem to be able to see you coming from a long distance (the Tewkesbury man must have radar eyes which see through trees), but they also appear to chat with each other to announce your arrival. I've known one become quite agitated when a boat did not turn up because it had stopped to picnic between locks.

It must be a lonely life, however, inhabiting these little cabins. Sometimes a man can sit there for hours, and nobody comes. One Severn lock-keeper occupies his time in making his cabin into a colourful profusion of flowers. But others just seem to sit and think. Or do they just sit?

Lockwheeling

I suppose the 'wheel' part comes from bicyles, but this term now seems to be used for anybody going ahead to get locks ready for boats, even if he is walking. Lockwheelers are in evidence where several locks are close together, in flights such as Napton, Tardebigge or Wigan. They amble on, making sure that each lock is full or empty as the case may be, and the gates open ready for the boat to go straight in. This is called 'setting' a lock. If the lock is already in the right shape the lockwheeler will say it is 'for' the boat; while if he has to work the paddles to change the water-level he will say it is 'against' the boat.

Obviously a bicycle is a useful device for this activity, and quite a few of the more cunning boaters carry one, either on the roof or ingeniously folded somewhere. The snag about using the roof is that low bridges sweep the cycle off. For less active lockwheelers there are midget motorised bikes. The great danger nowadays is that towpaths are not what they used to be. A crew member brandishing a windlass and pedalling along parts of the Shroppie or the Worcester-Birmingham, for example, may well meet a rock, a pothole, or just a gap, and end up in the cut instead of winding the next lot of paddle-gear.

Lockwheeling is a pleasant enough occupation, for you get plenty of time to lie down on broad balance-beams while the water runs in or out—though if you nod off your angry steerer may arrive and blast you awake again. Some lockwheelers, unfortunately, tend to forget that there may be a boat coming the other way. They drift blissfully on, setting lock after lock, until brought up short by a cross boat-crew from the other direction, wondering why a lock has suddenly been turned round in their faces.

Thus, idyllic as lockwheeling may be, you do need to peer over gates, or under bridges, or round corners before setting a lock, just in case somebody else is coming towards you. Possibly, if some stretches of waterway get any busier, we shall yet see old-fashioned fisticuffs between lockwheelers as in the old days.

Just for the record, a surprisingly enthusiastic body of waterway addicts around the almost lockless county of Sussex have banded together socially. And the name they picked for themselves was 'The Southern Lockwheelers'.

Lodes

'An open drain', says my dictionary about the word 'lode'—leaving one with a vision of sewage trapped between banks and attracting flies. But the lodes of the fenland waterways are hardly like that. They are 'drains', no doubt, like those magnificent waters of the Middle Level—and in fact some Middle Level branches are called lodes. But the lodes that most boaters come to sooner or later are the three which leave the River Cam at Upware.

They all start at one lock which seems to have a variety of names. In different publications it is called Upware Lock, Burwell Lock, Burwell Lode Lock, and Reach Lode Sluice. But there is only the one, though it has double gates at one end to allow for varying water-levels, and a guillotine at the other. And whatever its name, it takes you electrically to an intriguing parting of the ways.

To the left, under an ancient wooden bridge, you can follow a shallow channel up Wicken Lode, by the internationally-known nature reserve of Wicken Fen. This is not a wise trip for

large boats, but you can use the better centre route instead—Burwell Lode—and visit Adventurers' Fen from there. At the end of Burwell Lode is the village of Burwell, with a waterway alongside it like the cross of a letter T at the top of the Lode. This is $3\frac{3}{4}$ miles from the lock, past a brickworks and above the level of the fields. By the end the Lode is narrow and shallow for larger boats, but worth a mooring if you can make it.

The third lode is Reach Lode, straight as an arrow to Reach village 3 miles away. If you hope for a drink there you'll be unlucky, for there is no pub.

Neither Bottisham nor Swaffham, two other named lodes off the Cam, is now usable by cruisers. But there are other odd lodes on the Great Ouse system, and you might even cruise a short distance on Lakenheath Lode from the Little Ouse. If you leave your boat and walk, there are many lodes scattered about in this Fen area. Roll's Lode, Fenton Lode, Monk's Lode,

March

Yaxley Lode, Common Lode—but where is Salter's Lode, except as the name of a couple of notorious locks?

I leave it to historians to tell me the difference, if any, between a lode and a drain. For as far as I can see, Sam's Cut Drain, Grunty Fen Drain and Crooked Drain (for example) seem to do exactly the same job as (for example) Stake Lode, Methold Lode or High Lode. Come to think of it, is there any difference between the functions of either category and those of Lady Nunn's Old Eau, Well Creek, Beck Brook, Bevill's Leam, Pig Water, North Western Cut, Whittlesey Dyke, Old Pepper Lake, Old Hammond Beck, Old Croft River or the River Snail? They are all around those parts, busily draining away.

March

When I was a lad I knew the name of March as an important centre connected with the London & North Eastern Railway, and you will still see on the map five used or disused railways bearing down on it, as well as a mass of sidings.

Just how busy it is with trains now I don't know, but I know the town today in its lesser-known role as the heart and hub of the Middle Level Drains. These are the waterways below sea level, whose high banks hide wide vistas of sugar-beet being hoed, and where the only buildings you can see without standing on the roof are occasional leaning and sometimes deserted cottages, and a few pumping stations.

Most of the Drains are straight and wide, but through the centre of the whole 90-odd miles of them runs the meandering old course of the River Nene, and astride it sits March, whose motorists and railway travellers are almost certainly unaware of its waterway. Yet the Old Nene passes through what looks just like a Dutch canal snaking through a Dutch town. It is well below the level of the land, and the only main road bridge is so wide that most people do not realise that is is a bridge. But the waterway has its own secret March world, running along below pleasant gardens and a boatyard, and opposite a park.

If you emerge from the river into the town centre you may be taken aback by the traffic and the bustle, especially on market day. But there is good shopping here right across your route. Perhaps March seems to have little character by road, but it is a fine place to come to by water, especially as there is hardly any other collection of houses on the whole Middle Level once you've passed Whittlesey.

Marinas

The word 'marina' does not yet appear in dictionaries, but 'marine' means 'to do with the sea', since it is from the Latin for 'sea'. To use the word 'marina' on inland waterways, then, seems ridiculous, but it looks as if it is here to stay. It would be more sensible and pleasant, though, to use the word 'harbour', which means 'a refuge for boats'. And I still hope that future developers will call their refuges harbours.

Anyhow, whatever their name, these gatherings of boats alongside waterways seem to rouse strong feelings. Older enthusiasts talk sarcastically about 'boat-parks', and imply that here is a sort of motorway-mentality coming on to waterways. This seems to me a strange attitude, and I feel that what they are really saying is that they would rather not have all those boats on the waterways at all. For without the boat-parks the same boats would be moored in endless lines all along canals and rivers, most certainly destroying all pleasure for boaters, anglers and walkers alike, and looking like cars in London suburban streets.

An unspoken objection to marinas is that one has to pay to moor in them. Some people are funny about this. They happily invest several thousand pounds in a boat, then fall over themselves to avoid having to pay anyone for mooring it. If they can get away with it they will tie it to a tree somewhere, then complain bitterly if the local hooligans have broken into it, cast it adrift, or even—as has happened—set it on fire. Of course many people hate paying to park a car, so maybe this is some quirk of human nature.

For two reasons, then, surely boat-harbours are good ideas. They not only gather boats together where they have some greater degree of safety, but they also help to ensure that the waterways themselves are clear and peaceful for people to use.

There is one thing that needs to be said, however. It is important that any new harbours should be sited in sensible places. Some parts of our waterways have far too many moorings already, so that at weekends the surrounding waters and locks are in chaos. In one place, undoubtedly, the number of boatyards and marinas permitted nearby has led to lock closures. Yet there are great lengths of waterway, particularly near London, where there are no sizable moorings for boats at all.

The obvious places for new harbours are firstly well away from existing collections of boats, and secondly well away from possible bottlenecks such as flights of locks or narrow channels and heavily built-up areas. More harbours in the right places would be very welcome, and if there were enough of them this would help to keep mooring charges down.

There are several points which new developers (or for that matter some existing owners) might consider. If someone is paying to moor his boat, he will surely need, for example, his own reserved stretch of pier, so that he does not come back from a cruise and find someone else tied to it. He should be able to get there or leave without having to move other boats out of the way. He should be able to get near to his boat with his car, so that he does not have to lug things for long distances. There should be somewhere to leave the car itself in safety. Fuel and water-points should be easily accessible and not always cluttered up with other boats. There should be rubbish and toilet-disposal points, competent repair services, and winter facilities.

The whole aesthetic idea of a mass of boats gathered together in this way is certainly distasteful. But to my mind it is far less distasteful than to have 2000 miles of waterway lined with boats, bouncing into each other as everyone else passes, some sinking, some abandoned for ever, many with covers adrift in the breeze. Linear moorings can become the major eyesores of our waterways.

Mattresses

Country-dwellers know only too well the tribe of morons who drive out from towns at week-ends with pensioned-off mattresses strapped to their roof-racks. They look for a pleasant and lonely stretch of countryside and dump them into roadside hedges. Sometimes they bring the bedstead as well!

What is not so well-known except to canal travellers is that other urban dwellers, either without cars or without the urge to travel right into the country, merely carry their old mattresses to the nearest canal and drop them over a bridge. Thus, sooner or later, some unfortunate boater gets them tangled in his propeller.

Foam rubber mattresses are not so bad, since the propeller can sometimes chop through them, and they are not so difficult to get off unless they have a really tough binding around their edges. But coiled-spring mattresses are another thing. I once collected one on the River Nene (unusual on a river) which took half-an-hour to cut off with wire-cutters. But one I picked up on the Caldon Canal luckily hung on by a strap, and merely trailed along the canal bed without offering its coils to my propeller. I wound up a certain amount of spring once at one of those narrow 'nips' in the BCN, but the engine stopped in time to prevent too much of a tangle.

It is certainly wise to carry wire-cutters—and not only for spring mattresses. And there's a great advantage in having either an outboard engine or an outdrive which will come up out of the water so that you can lie in comfort to do your wire-cutting.

One awkward problem arises on finding one of these things in a waterway—quite apart from the insoluble problem of trying to stop people throwing them in: when you have cut it off your propeller, what do you do with it? It is usually too heavy and waterlogged even to get on to the bank. But if you can land it, there is hardly a place to put it where it will not soon be thrown back again. And the mattress-tossing powers of some people, even well away from bridges, are unbelievable.

May blossom

I often think that May is the finest month to cruise, and I always associate maytree blossom with these marvellous spring journeys. With luck there is fine weather, the days are long, the brilliant greens of spring have not yet turned to dull uniformity, and there is a tremendous amount of flower about.

Hawthorn, or may, seems very fond of some waterways. It forms towpath hedges, at 10ft high or more, and the opposite banks may well be lined for miles with vast bushes, hanging over the water and providing nesting-places for moorhens along their lower branches.

After a mild winter there are a couple of weeks in May when

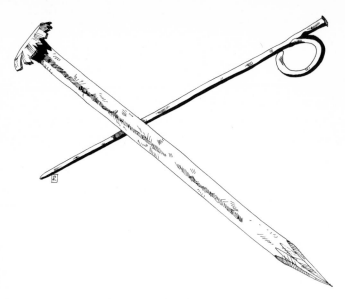

you never seem to be out of sight or scent of the hawthorn blossom. A long stretch of the Grand Union around Gayton is especially thick with it. It is one of the several specialities of the River Nene, and the Lancaster and the Brecon & Abergavenny offer you tastes of it. It is a heady scent, and a wonderful snowy sight, but you have to catch it at the right moment or it has gone.

Mooring pins

On the Broads it is fashionable to secure your boat with those awkward things called rond anchors, which I find extremely difficult to get into the ground, and not very secure when they are in. I have also met them on the Brecon & Abergavenny Canal. But most people on inland waterways use things known as mooring pins or mooring spikes. These are solid rods of metal, maybe 18in long, with a point at the bottom and a reinforced top for knocking in with a heavy hammer. You clout them into the bank, leaning them at a slight angle away from your boat, then drop a quick neat knot over them—though the appropriate type of knot still seems to be a matter of argument among boaters.

It is always intriguing to discover that beneath a grass-covered towpath there often lurks a much more solid foundation, and sometimes a mooring pin will refuse to penetrate this rock-like slab of history. So you try a few other spots, until presumably you find a weakness in the original towpath, and your pin goes in. It sometimes stays in so hard and fast then that you have difficulty getting it out again; one of mine once came out so suddenly that I needed a stitch in my eyelid in a Rugby hospital.

One type of mooring pin without much reinforcement to its head develops a lethal rim of bent-over metal after a few months of bashing, and this can take pieces out of your hands if you do not handle it with respect. And if you economise by getting rather slim pins you will certainly bend them under your hammering along the tougher towpaths.

Like other vital boating tools such as windlasses, it is always safest to have a few spare pins with you, for they have a habit of being left behind, or jumping off your deck if dropped from a height. Your hammer, too, can be left in the long grass, and you will never get the pins into the ground without it. If you do happen to lose a hammer, there is no need to find a chandlery. Try the nearest ironmonger's for I discovered that they are sold there—in Oldbury, anyhow—under the name of 'lump hammers'.

Names

Uncle Ben's Bridge, believe it or not, is next to a pub kept by an Indian landlord on the highest level of the Birmingham Canal Navigations. Pudding Green I mention elsewhere in this book. Then there are the two Bumbleholes, one on the Staffs & Worcs and one south of Netherton tunnel. There is Grub Street cutting—mysterious, secret and tropical on the Shropshire Union, and Anton's Gowt, also elsewhere in this book. The Staffs & Worcs again—surely the most fertile—has Giggetty,

Wombourn, Dimmingsdale and Bratch in addition to its Bumblehole.

It seems to me that the waterway system has a greater proportion of odd names scattered around than those on our roads. Many belong to bridges, where canal builders may have been pressed to think of enough names. And maybe the BCN beats the Staffs & Worcs here, for I recall bridges named Bughole, Gillity, Jolly Collier, Sneyd Junction, Adam & Eve, Devils Elbow, Olinthus, Cuckoo, Thimblemill Lane, and Whimsey, not to mention Spouthouse Aqueduct. There is Old Man's Bridge on the Chesterfield, with a man's gnarled face on it in stone, and on the Gloucester-Sharpness Canal they believe in such terse names as Splatt, Cam, Rea, Patch and Sims. But where did Blackburn get such bridge names as Side Beet, Sour Milk Hall and Paradise, giving it a good start in the Leeds & Liverpool league, despite names elsewhere on that canal such as Clogger, Tottleworth, Cockshott, Dawbers, Stegneck, Swine Lane, Dubb and (lovely!) Milking Hill?

I seem to have got stuck with bridges, for of course they are the main items along waterways, which tend to touch very few villages and thus miss the pleasures of Sixpenny Handley, Tolpuddle and Piddletrenthide. There's Husbands Bosworth and, not far away, Crick, and I suppose Wyrley & Essington is a fine musical name for a canal itself. Then the Shropshire Union has some pleasant place-names such as Brewood (which you call Brood), Wheaton Aston, Gnosall (which some call Nawzle) and Bunbury, with Cholmondeston and Wimboldsley on its Middlewich branch.

Musical names and ugly names (there actually is an Ugly bridge in the Hatton flight), mysterious names and almost unbelievable names—take your pick. I cannot decide on my own favourite, since I keep coming across new ones. I think Billy Tight's Swing Bridge on the Macclesfield is high on my list, though it is a pity that it is so difficult for us to get to Old Sod House lock on the Market Weighton Canal.

Navvies

I suppose there are still people who do not know the origin of this word. It came from the chaps who gouged out our canals with spades and wheelbarrows and muscles, long before draglines and excavators were thought of. Canal-makers were, by some curious derivation from the sea, called 'navigators', and ever since the shortened word has been applied to any breed of muscular chap heaving earth about and getting in a sweat.

The wheel has come round, in fact, for once more the canals and rivers have been invaded by an army of twentieth-century navvies. But this time they come for love and not pay, and at least they have the help of machines at times. These are the boys and girls (of all ages) who enjoy their weekends up to their waists in mud in a derelict lock, or dragging out old prams, cookers, washing-machines, bedsteads and motor-cycles from an urban canal dumping-ground, or heaving out bushes and trees to reveal a long-hidden towpath.

People of all sorts come from a variety of sources to join working-parties from the Pocklington to the Kennet & Avon, from the Basingstoke to the Montgomeryshire. In all weathers and at all times of year they come, from canal societies and youth clubs, from Trusts and Associations, from boating clubs and from nowhere in particular. But mostly they have a loose federal-like link with the incredible Waterway Recovery Group, which co-ordinates much of this navvying.

The group is the baby of jovial bearded Graham Palmer, a man who believes in cutting cackle and getting down to the horses—or more likely to the bottom of a lock. At the same time the WRG administratively sorts out an incredible variety of working-parties, restoration projects, revivals and mere cleanings-up. Just to meet a gang of its red-shirted enthusiasts would stir some sort of response from a corpse.

If ever any group of people looked as if they really enjoyed life, the WRG supporters do. There must be a moral in this somewhere, for the state they get themselves into would in theory deter anybody else from joining them. But it seems to be a disease: the deeper the mud, the greater the tonnage of dragged-out affluent-society junk; the heavier the downpour, the higher their spirits seem to rise. So they take their blisters and their mud, and sluice themselves at the current camp or village hall, ready for a mighty sing-song to round off the day.

If you don't know of this new race, get hold of their magazine, *Navvies.* Before you can turn round you'll be sending them your Green Shield stamps towards a new excavator, then following up in person and heaving out old motor-cars with the best of them. Certainly whole lengths of deeper and clearer channels, walkable towpaths, and especially stretches of restored rivers and canals would not be there without today's enthusiastic navvies.

The old navvies used to frighten the lives out of the local population. The new ones might alarm you a bit when you first come across them. But when you get to know them, they're an extremely lovable lot. Oh, and by the way, they may well be solicitors or doctors when they wear their other hats.

Nene river

This, I must confess, is my favourite river, yet most people give a groan when you mention it. They groan, apparently, because of the 37 locks (there is a 38th at Dog-in-a-Doublet, *qv*, out to the tidal section).

It is a debatable point whether the numerous smooth, if wide, turns to open a guillotine-gate on the Nene are any more exhausting than the back-breaking struggles sometimes needed even to make a start on opening a paddle elsewhere. But it is certainly true that turning a big handle 156 times at Northampton or Rush Mills, and a rather smaller number of times at the other Nene locks, uses a great deal of energy. All the same, your reward is a lovely, winding, peaceful river, with wide views across water-meadows to little villages and churches on the foothills. Hardly anything creeps in—tree, hedge or building—to block your view.

This is how the Nene, with its wide-open panorama, grips you. No doubt the lack of buildings on its banks is due to its

nasty flooding habits, which in turn gave rise to these massive gates to control the floods. But in spring especially, when the may-blossom is out, there is wonderful relaxation in drifting through these meadows towards the next lock-guillotine, which seems to shift itself about in the distance.

All the locks have ordinary top gates and these guillotine-gates at their bottom ends; most are vertical but three are curved. And since the gates must normally be left up, you have the job of closing them at first and opening them afterwards, whichever way you are moving along the river—which of course doubles the number of turns each time. Yet somehow the inch-by-inch movement of the guillotine-gate has never bothered me as it apparently bothers some. Maybe it's because I'm watching the cattle. Yes, I must not forget the Nene cattle, which seem to inhabit the riverside fields in huge numbers, interspersed only now and again by flocks of sheep. Wherever you stop, except for the few towns near to the river, herds of inquisitive bullocks come galloping from nowhere to look at you. They snuffle and trample and barge each other about, and even drool down your windows. And really this is the only small warning I might issue to potential Nene visitors: do not worry about the locks, but if you don't like cattle, keep away, for you will have difficulty in finding a cattle-free mooring—and for that matter, a cattle-free lock. Maybe I am exaggerating, but that is the impression I had.

As for the towns, even they are reluctant to place buildings on the river's banks. Northampton, Wellingborough and Peterborough have trees, mown grass and flowers waiting for you. Oundle stays even further away, and rests inside a vast horseshoe bend, with a fair walk to the shops from either arm. Peterborough's fine moorings I have mentioned elsewhere. As for the villages, they prefer to stay near the foothills, and you have a gentle walk to find a pub. But the pubs are there, and some offer some pleasant food as well.

The Nene has to be cruised to be believed. There are 17 narrow locks from the Grand Union to get there, and you have to make arrangements and pay fees in order to have keys waiting for you at the Northampton toll house to enable you to work the locks. Then unless you are going through the Middle Level to the Great Ouse you have to come all the way back again. But it is a wonderful journey—provided you do not expect to get through every lock in five minutes flat.

Nips

Around the Trent and on the Chesterfield Canal I have heard this term used to name narrow places on waterways; it is certainly short, sharp and accurate, so I will borrow it. For narrow places, on canals anyhow, are both intriguing and sometimes hazardous.

There's that troublesome length towards the top end of the Llangollen, for example, where the canal is high above the Dee and a rocky stretch keeps it so narrow that two boats could not possibly pass. Yet unfortunately there is a bend, so that two can be approaching each other without knowing this at first. There must be many an argument along here, and much unplanned practice in the difficult art of steering backwards.

There is a similar long nip just north of Wolverhampton on the Staffs & Worcs. Again, you cannot always see if another boat has started to navigate it from the other end, but in this case there are one or two passing-places dug out in the side, so that it is not necessary to reverse for long distances. There are a few shorter nips on the Shropshire Union, and in some of the Shroppie cuttings passing is very difficult. At Wilmcote on the southern Stratford there is another short and curving stretch where passing is impossible.

These nips are not as tight as the width of a narrow boat, but are merely places too narrow for two boats to be alongside one another. True nips are those of 7ft wide; chief among them are obviously locks, which are the features that decide the maximum width of anything passing through the waterway. Normal width canal boats just fit between the walls, whereas bulging craft, or those with dangling fenders, get themselves jammed there. Walls in locks might have bulged, so that perfectly good boats have stuck in them; and that is why the use of fenders in narrow locks is asking for trouble. It is a good lock that stays the same width everywhere.

Most boaters realise that when passing through nips they are bound to scrape the sides—though it is surprising how many people get agitated about touching even the sides of a lock. But any boat to be used on canals must have sturdy and vertical sides, or at least rubbing strakes to protect them.

The most vigorous scrapings occur not so much at locks, where you are hardly moving, but when passing under way through some other form of nip—Stratford Canal bridges, for example. And there is that other odd bridge near Barton-under-Needwood, mentioned elsewhere, where knobbly metal lumps catch your sides just when you think you are getting away scot-free. (The same Trent & Mersey metal knobs are to be found on the walls of nearby locks).

Unexpected nips when you are still at normal cruising speed also occur where bridges have been removed, and you might not realise until the last minute that the canal suddenly narrows. Although I mentioned especially the Stratford bridges, which have no towpath under them, hundreds of bridges on narrow canals have a water-channel only just wide enough for a narrow boat, though the bridge itself extends over a towpath as well. This makes steering tricky, since you tend to steer through the middle of the arch, but even if you avoid this trap, some bridges are especially treacherous because the outer slope of the bridge may catch you, even if there is a little spare space in the water channel.

One other thing remains to be said about bridge-nips. Many are on blind bends, and canal-cruising can still be so peaceful that you forget about other boats. Then, just as you triumphantly pass through without touching the sides, another boat comes towards you making for the same bridge-hole. Thus blind bridge-nips call not only for careful steering, but also for hooter-sounding and speed-reduction.

Particularly tricky nips are the long aqueducts, and in some cases tunnels, barely the width of the boat. The Pontcysyllte and the Edstone, on a windy day, challenge anyone to cross them without grinding the sides most of the way. And the tunnels at Chirk and Curdworth, for example, echo to your scrunches as you gingerly move through. It is always a delicate business deciding just how slowly you can go to minimise scraping, without losing effective steering control.

Then there are those famous BCN nips—islands where the toll-houses used to stand, and where you now slide through with your heart in your mouth in case somebody has dropped an old motor-car in. There's one on the main line where the towpath infuriatingly curves in as you leave, making it difficult to manoeuvre yourself away from it and out into the channel again. Since the toll-houses stood on islands, there were passages on either side; only one has been dredged now, and sometimes there is doubt as to which one it is.

There are few lengths on the narrow canals where you are not going to be nipped in some way or other, by lock, bridge, aqueduct, tunnel, cutting or old toll-point. If you travel such canals, trust in a steel hull or metal-capped rubbing strakes. If you trust only in fenders you may find yourself nipped to a standstill.

Norfolk Broads

In some ways waterway boaters are of three types, who rarely intermingle. There are the wide-ranging travellers, whose wanderings also include linked rivers such as the Trent, Severn, Avon, Lee and Stort; there are the users of the Thames who never seem to leave that river or work a lock on their own; and there are those who cruise on the Broads.

The Norfolk and Suffolk Broads (yes, don't forget Suffolk) are certainly out on a limb. Anybody afloat at York, Liverpool, Gloucester, Birmingham, Bishop's Stortford or Guildford can cruise to all the other places named and many more, but people afloat at Wroxham or Great Yarmouth are stuck with the Ant, the Bure, the Chet, the Yare and the Waveney for the rest of their lives. And never can they cross to the other 2000-odd miles of waterways.

They seem, then, a race apart. Yet in themselves they vary astonishingly. At one end of the spectrum are dedicated sailing people, sweeping about the wide broads or tacking painfully up narrow rivers, and merely rippling the water, but pestered most of the year by the motor-cruisers at the other end of the spectrum, growling everywhere like herds of elephants.

Maybe none of the Broads users envies other waterways. For though they never hear the ringing clatter of a paddle-rack or the whirl of water in a lock, and never have the satisfaction of lying flat on a balance-beam, before pushing gently on it, they also never meet the delights of an old pram wrapped round their propeller, or a sunken motor-car scraping their keel. They do not have to strain their way laboriously up a shallow channel in the centre of a very narrow and winding waterway, or indeed find a pound between locks with no water in it at all.

Admittedly, however, they might find themselves in a procession of boats stretching as far as the eye can see, and though the banks may be deep enough to get near compared

97

with those along canals, they might discover that those banks are already thickly lined with boats.

Boats on the Broads have an advantage over those on canals: they can be wider. This means that there is room to swing a cat round between the cabin sides, instead of being squeezed to a 7ft width and only being able to expand fore and aft. Nor do the Broads boats—in theory anyway—need all round protection against bridges, lock-gates and jagged things sticking out of lock-walls. But this is perhaps cancelled out by their urgent need for protection against other boats.

For despite the apparent relaxation of being able to cruise along wide, deep waterways and extensive broads, compared with the hazards of navigating shallow winding canals, the comparison is not straightforward. The very ease of Broads cruising has led not only to gross overcrowding in places, but also to the appearance of irresponsible people who ought never to be allowed on boats at all.

So at times you feel not only that you have exchanged the motorway for a comparable boatway, but you also find yourself contending with high-spirited boatloads of transistor-wielding, beer-can-throwing, airgun-firing yobboes, who don't mind how many other boats they cannon off in their progress through the crowds.

You may be lucky enough to miss this sort of thing, and of course you are not compelled to use only the moorings at pubs and village centres. There are still long empty stretches of waterway available. But the fact remains that despite the harder work and greater problems of canal cruising, you will find a remarkable number of canallers who are refugees from the Broads, never to return.

Nottingham

I think Nottingham probably deserves a pat on the back in regard to its waterways, though I do not know how much is due to the local council and how much to British Waterways. But a few years ago people regarded the necessary canal passage

through the city, to get from Beeston on the Trent to Meadow
Lane on the Trent, as a sort of unavoidable evil. It took in
shallow, evil-coloured, junk-filled channels, and for long
distances the banks were a continuous rubbish-dump, with great
sheets of polythene blowing across to snarl your propeller.

There seemed to be nowhere to moor, for at the one likely
place below Castle Lock were off-putting notices to stop you
from hammering mooring-pins into the towpath. Thus
everyone was greatly relieved to thread a last delicate way past
the boats at Meadow Lane and out into the wide river again.

Much of this has changed. The waterway has been cleared of
rubbish, and many acres of the dumps have been grassed over to

99

make pleasant surroundings. The towpath has been cut back and cleared, and altogether the whole journey is far more relaxing and salubrious than it used to be. The castle rears up in front of you, there are boats here and there, and although the gloomy turn under the bridges towards Meadow Lane remains, everything seems so much tidier.

Things can change again rapidly, I know, and there is still room for some decent official moorings along the canal. But you can always turn upriver under Trent Bridge, and moor magnificently under the shadow of County Hall and the Bridgford Hotel—one of the finest stopping-places anywhere.

All the same, even if things move backwards a little, thank you to those people who in the last few years have transformed the canal journey from what it used to be. Let us now look forward to some high-level decisions that will make Nottingham the busy river-port it ought to have become long ago.

Old cars

One of the less pleasant memories of cruising on inland waterways is the number of wrecked cars encountered. The side of canals seems an especial favourite for car graveyards. Offhand I remember a mountain of cars at Loughborough, a smaller pile in Nottingham, a battered-looking collection on the way to Salford Bridge in Birmingham, and dozens of other garage and factory backyards where discarded vehicles have been dumped.

Despite growing awareness in most communities that a waterway can be a pleasant asset, too many people still regard their canal bank boundary as a rubbish tip, supposedly out of sight. Worse are firms which feel that strips of land along waterways can be used for the less salubrious activities of mankind. Thus a cruise through built-up areas today alternates between increasing numbers of neat places which people can enjoy, and the remaining eyesores liberally littered with junk.

The snag about old cars on waterway banks is that they can easily be pushed in, and quite a few are. Any firm piling its banks with mounds of rubbish should be made to erect a strong fence to contain it.

A heap of old cars on the bank gives the boater fair warning to pass with care. But old cars in other places are not always so obvious. I have seen many spots where a waterway has blatantly been used to get rid of a wreck by pushing it down a convenient slope. If you are lucky, it ends up well to the side and clearly visible partly above water, like one or two near Bedworth and another at Alperton. But others go further in and hide themselves dangerously in the deeper channel.

Every regular waterway user has tales of meeting cars with the bottom of his hull, and more than once I have heard of cars in locks. Those people who wax indignant about old cars dumped by roadsides really don't know what they're missing. At least they cannot go aground on one in the middle of the road.

Oxclose Lock

This lock on the Ripon Canal has one claim to fame. It is the northernmost lock on the whole linked waterway network of England. The Tewitfield locks on the isolated Lancaster just beat it until they were savagely deleted, but it now reigns alone.

It takes some reaching, though, for you have all the complications of the tidal Yorkshire Ouse, even if you wisely come round by the Selby Canal. The sad thing is that if you think hopefully of cruising to Ripon you will be disappointed. The remaining two locks on this canal are closed, and in fact the whole thing was only just over 2 miles long to start with. Now only $1\frac{1}{4}$ miles remain navigable. Moreover, navigation rights were legally removed in 1955, but fortunately the Ripon Motor Boat Club moors there and guards the $1\frac{1}{4}$ miles with care. And Oxclose is in good condition.

It is an interesting lock: there is a notice pointing out that the 'clews' must be left shut—a curious spelling of what is normally written 'cloughs' (and pronounced 'clows'); and there are sturdy footplanks across the top gate, with parts which must be

Peat

hinged up when the gates are opened in order to clear the ground paddles. The bottom gates should be left open, and you could easily miss the entrance to the lock from the River Ure. If you did, however, you would soon know about it.

The Boat Club flourishes, but it must get few visitors from the distant world of other canals, which is a pity, for this is lovely country, and Ripon itself is worth the walk.

Peat

Peat is closely associated with water, and there are said to be eight million acres of peat-covered land in the British Isles. The rich soils around the Fenland waterways contain much of it, and as you stand on your roof in the Middle Level you can see crops sprouting lusciously from the black fields.

Canals are not likely to pass through peaty areas, but curiously enough the Llangollen runs near celebrated peat land called Whixall Moss—an odd remote part with interesting flowers and insects. The canal is raised above the level of the

Peterborough

land, and there is an eerie look about the surroundings. If you explore the district on the towpath side you might well come across peat blocks drying, for peat has been sold from here for many years. The Macclesfield Canal, too, curves round by Dane's Moss just south of Macclesfield, and the old BW guide talks of peat-cutting there.

Peterborough

To most people this town is a soulless expanding collection of buildings and vehicles, channelling all its traffic to one bridge over the River Nene. To boaters down that river it was, until recently, an unwelcoming place, where they nervously tried to find precarious moorings, only to discover that it was almost impossible to get anywhere near the bank. There was one spot by the railway bridge where you could insalubriously tie up, and there was supposed to be a town quay, but this always seemed to be blocked by something.

Now all this has changed, and seemingly at a stroke Peterborough offers some of the finest moorings in the country. In a great sweep over a mile long below the road bridge, and alongside trees and grass, are bollards and rings in a profusion unmatched anywhere, with the proper depth of water to hold an armada. Nor are the bollards those pathetic little pegs or concrete posts which go by that name elsewhere. This new generation may not match the monsters along the locksides upriver, but they are pretty solid metal devices all the same.

There they stretch into the distance, with rings between to allow for shorter boats, so that you can tie up in comfort and sunbathe on the grass of the park alongside. There are litter bins handy—though possibly not put there with boats in mind—and the shops are little more than a stone's throw away if you can manage to cross a couple of roads without being mown down. The only little extra that would make this a perfect mooring-place would be an occasional water-tap, for the Nene is very short of them.

Whoever master-minded this development deserves a niche of honour in waterway cruising circles. Too many towns care nothing about their watersides, or about the boats which visit them. They remove none of the rubbish thrown in by their ratepayers, and offer no pleasant water's edge where boats can tie up and the same ratepayers can walk enjoyably. Next time you come across a town neglecting its waterway frontage, ship its councillors to see the moorings of Peterborough. They may not be able to emulate the squat but fascinating cathedral across the park, but they could certainly learn a lesson from the waterside.

Potter Heigham

This is a revered name in Broadland, though the place is not what it was. Here, for many years, Herbert Woods built boats, and countless thousands of people have come to hire both motor cruisers and sailing boats. Nowadays you can hardly breathe in summer for a pulsating mass of people, cars, and boats on land and on water around the boatyard.

Potter Heigham is also notorious among Broads users, for here is the most awkward bridge on the whole Broads system. And because boats here are not limited in their size by such items as narrow locks, hirers have made them bigger and fatter through the years. But always they have had to keep a wary eye on Potter Heigham bridge. The result is that boatyards everywhere offer boats which will clear it by about one inch at each edge of the roof.

Few people feel qualified to shoot a bridge—especially in a cross-wind—which only gives an inch clearance. So the main hiring agencies have felt compelled to provide pilots merely for the shooting of Potter Heigham bridge. And incredible chaps they are. They cast an eye on your boat—which they probably know by heart anyway—and will tell you straight away whether it will make it or not. Having made their decision they leap aboard, take your controls, and pop you through without batting an eyelid, though you are convinced all the way that they will knock pieces off the boat.

Some boats, of course, do knock pieces off themselves, as the sharply-sloping sides of the bridge clearly show. But if you want to see a living example of the camel-through-the-eye-of-a-needle act, go and watch Potter Heigham bridge at the height of the season.

Pudding Green

Pudding Green has always fascinated me as a name, and yet I have never troubled to set foot ashore and see what it means to its inhabitants. No doubt there are some, and maybe there are shops and pubs as well as houses. Maybe they even play cricket there in summer, with rooks building in the trees round about and the occasional sleepy click of the ball.

Somehow I doubt this last fantasy, for Pudding Green is the name of a junction on the main line of the Birmingham Canal Navigations. And since it is somewhere between Oldbury,

Smethwick and West Bromwich I think I must dismiss the village green dream that the name tends to arouse.

In case you do not know it and would like to locate it, PG is 5 miles 3 furlongs from Farmers Bridge in Birmingham, via the New Main line; or (surprise) only 5 miles via the Old Line—excluding the loops but of course including the Smethwick 3 locks and the Spon Lane 3 (maybe the oldest in England?). Or if you come from Wolverhampton it is $9\frac{3}{4}$ miles from Aldersley Junction, plus 24 locks. If you wish to go there from Stourton on the Staffs & Worcs it is exactly 14 miles (plus 29 locks) via Netherton tunnel. Or you can use Dudley tunnel instead if you have a low enough boat, with legging your way through. It is then only 12 miles 7 furlongs from Stourton via Factory Junction (35 locks), or 13 miles and a $\frac{1}{2}$ furlong via Brades Hall with the same number of locks. And there are other permutations, including the Soho Loop, the Icknield Port Loop and the Oozells Street Loop if you feel so inclined.

The thing about Pudding Green is that it is the junction where you turn up to reach the northern wanderings of the BCN. There are nine other junctions on the Main Line alone, so make sure you get the right one. If you do, you go off at an angle towards West Bromwich and then down 8 locks to a low bridge before you reach the wasteland around the power station where the Tame Valley Canal comes in. Then there is a long drawn-out stretch to Walsall, and 8 locks up to another distinctive power station at Birchills on the Wyrley & Essington Canal.

This is the interesting northern fringe of the BCN. To the right you reach the narrow boats of Norton Canes, and later Anglesey Basin in its remoteness. To the left you sweep back to Wolverhampton again, mooring at Rough Wood if you can get in.

It is all a long way from Pudding Green, and I apologise to the inhabitants for never getting off and having a look at them (though often, with canals, the inhabitants themselves do not know a canal is there). But I think of Pudding Green—village cricket or not—as being at the hub of the BCN; as a junction though it is about as unmemorable as it could possibly be.

Puddle

This word is in the singular because there are two kinds along canals—one in the singular only, and one that can be plural as well.

The singular-or-plural one is the common kind, always found at infuriating places. It tends to develop alongside paddle gear and in a curve following the end of a balance-beam. Such puddles are formed by generations of feet, standing and moving to work the paddles and open the gates respectively. For days after a shower you have to carry out these operations in a pair of gumboots, unless you want mud over the tops of your boating-shoes at every lock. And to make matters worse, the curved puddles under the balance-beams make marvellous skid-pans, just when you are struggling to get the maximum leverage from your heels to start the beam moving.

This problem is solved at many locks by the provision of concrete slabs or wooden platforms by the paddle gear, and ridged tracks of brick or concrete following the swing of the balance-beam. But somehow I am not sure I wouldn't rather have the grass-lined puddles than some of those naked stretches of concrete.

The other type of canal puddle is the name given to the stuff you cannot see, which forms the lining of the canal bed. When canals were dug, most had to be lined to stop the water vanishing through the bottom. This was done with a mixture of clay and water, and, perhaps, sand, put down in several layers and trodden in laboriously by the navvies for hour after hour, reminiscent of the traditional method of producing wine. I am also told that in places a flock of sheep would be driven up and down by a dog instead.

The result has been remarkably effective, and although the puddle is now covered everywhere by generations of silt and old bedsteads, it still valiantly keeps the water in. You can often see its present-day counterpart in maintenance-boats when odd

Push-tug

bits of the canal are being repaired—though I have not seen anybody treading it in.

An ironic—or is it ingenious?—sign of progress is the latest suggestion that large sheets of polythene, suitably anchored and covered, could in future do the same job. I would like to hear Brindley's comment.

Push-tugs

This strikes me as a rather curious name, for the essential thing about tugs is surely that they tug—which according to my dictionary means 'pull sharply and roughly; haul, pull hard'. How then can a thing called a tug have the word 'push' stuck on to its name?

Presumably, however, this weird name was coined to describe a vessel which can either push OR tug—in which case a better name would have been 'Push-or-tug'. Anyhow, these are the things you are liable to come across on the broad Yorkshire canals, pushing (or perhaps even tugging) containers full of coal to power stations, or BACAT barges to BACAT ships.

The pushing part seems to be an odd idea on the face of it. If you have a string of floating containers, the obvious thing to the layman is to pull them along in a train, as the Tom Pudding boats have been pulled for many years. But presumably there is a technical reason why you can join a few containers together more rigidly and put a power unit behind them, making the whole thing into a sort of very long boat, driven and steered from the back. In fact, the push-tug seems to be nothing more than a floating engine-cum-rudder, with the driver perched high up in order to see over the mounds of coal in front of him.

The steerers seem perfectly happy to tug instead of push—at least when their train is empty—and I have seen one come skidding under the North Road bridge at Ferrybridge, heading for the lock, for all the world as if he was on the Silverstone racetrack. The compartment boats, incidentally, ride alarmingly high in the water after they have been yanked out and emptied of their coal.

If you happen to see these boats being loaded at Kellingley colliery it is a remarkable sight. The coal is poured into one end of each boat first, so that the thing tips up at a dangerous-looking angle. But by the time the other end has been filled, and then the middle, there is not much boat left above the water-line.

Push-tugs at least look exceptionally up-to-date on our waterways, and although they cannot follow the French habit of carrying their own cars on board, I have certainly seen one with a motor-scooter.

Racks

'Rack', I am told by the technically-minded, is the official name to give to that row of teeth, stuck on a vertical slab of metal, which is then connected by a rod to the paddle-shutter below the water at most locks—except that some racks are horizontal on the Leeds & Liverpool. Your windlass turns the cogs which engage these teeth, thus enabling the shutter to be opened.

Now the great thing about racks—the vertical type anyway—is that you can see from afar whether they are up or down. When they are up the paddle is open, and when they are

Rack: Leeds & Liverpool

down it is closed. And boaters soon get into the habit of looking
ahead at a lock—even through binoculars—to see whether it is
ready or not. When you are working the gear, too, you can see
from the movement of the rack whether you are winding the
right way or not. And as the rack rises you know your paddle is
opening. Even more important, it is easy to look back as you
leave a lock and check whether you have left a paddle up or not.

Sadly, however, despite their useful attributes, visible racks
seem to be falling out of favour. Instead the canals in particular
are acquiring a collection of mysterious contraptions designed to
make work easier for the weakest canaller, but to flummox us

all properly at the same time.

The mechanism on these new devices is entirely enclosed, and no doubt this helps to keep the rust away. But unless you have remembered your spectacles you have to peer very closely to discover whether the paddle is up, down, or midway, and even which way to turn your windlass. You certainly cannot fathom anything from a few feet away, and there is nothing from the distance to show whether you have left a paddle up or not.

So although flabby-muscled boaters may prefer the easier work of the new-fangled gear, I'll bet it leads to many a lowered pound. Old stagers criticise it for just these practical reasons, as well as for their sentimental attachment to the lovable, greasy, rising, easily-visible racks of old.

Rallies

A delicate subject. Boaters are either rallying kinds or not, and I'm not. I tend to use a boat for cruising rather than for mooring with 500 other boats and being sociable. But I grant the ralliers their points, which seem to be two. Firstly, boat rallies over the years have played a tremendous part in bringing waterways into the public eye and back into use. And secondly, a rally is a fine way of meeting all the friends that you last met at the previous one and will meet again at the next.

Each year there are more and more rallies, and maybe soon there will be so many that the rest of the waterways will be empty for most of the time for the rest of us to cruise along. With careful planning the devoted rallier can leapfrog his way all over England from rally to rally, until his boat is so loaded with rally plaques that it draws several inches more water—which is all to the good of the channel.

One intriguing aspect of rallies is the increasing number of attractions which seem to have nothing at all to do with boats or waterways. Fair organs, hot-air balloons, parachutists, Scottish dancers, handbell ringers, weavers, pig-roasts—it is surprising that the public has a moment to spare for the waterway and the boats.

Rally: Oxford

The boats too have their variety. The true narrow boats are always there in strength, and in harmony with smaller outboard-driven boats. But there are several unusual boats. There are bound to be one or two steam-driven craft, including the incredible little paddle-wheeler from the Brecon & Abergavenny Canal, and no doubt John Player's *Hero*, too. Then there may be that small cruiser with a sort of Nissen-hut butty, which I am told is used as a dog-kennel. There is usually a well-known inflatable which will have been rowed for some way to get there, and undoubtedly there will be one of those enterprising Ashby Canal coal boats, busily shovelling coal into bags to sell.

Capella will be there, with a variety of waterway painted ware. One or two boats will have Heath Robinson propulsion systems, and inevitably there will be an imitation destroyer and/or submarine (but see ROYAL NAVY).

The problems of organising a rally are formidable, not least in the fields of rubbish-disposal, bread-providing, water-supply, and toilets. But there never seems to be a shortage of keen volunteers for all aspects of the work. And though when everybody has gone the site sometimes looks like the aftermath of a hurricane, a rally certainly makes a strong local impression—usually for the good where there has been local authority apathy.

It may be that there are now too many rallies, and that the whole business has got out of hand. Some people think that the big national rallies have become far too bloated, and outgrown their original purpose. But like caravanners, there will continue to be boaters who regard their rallies as the highlights of their season's boating. Good luck to them—though the people I'm sorry for are the unfortunate first-time boat hirers who find themselves having to steer through a rally site on their first day out.

Royal Navy

This may seem a curious topic for an inland waterways book, but few regular inland boaters will have failed to meet some odd boats apparently belonging to the Navy. Looking like vast cardboard models from an industrious school handicrafts project, they pretend to be two guided missile destroyers, a frigate and a submarine, but built to fit the seven-foot locks of the narrow canals. Nelson must be having a terrible time in his grave, but seemingly these four vessels are not in fact the total remaining complement of the Royal Navy, but merely a method of recruiting for the real ships.

Both ex-naval men and enthusiastic inland waterway users have been heard to express horror at the sight of these neither-fish-nor-fowl boats. But there is no doubt that they are a great attraction to the public, whatever sailors or protesting taxpayers may feel. Queues of children shuffle through them wherever they go. And whether they actually recruit anybody or not, they are certainly as popular as the clowns at the circus. The Ministry of Defence must be proud of them.

Shear-pins

Owners of boats propelled by certain types of outboard motors often carry little boxes about with them containing ten or a dozen short, round lengths of metal known as shear-pins. They serve one simple purpose, to make sure that the boat is not stuck in the middle of nowhere with a propeller that will not turn.

No propeller, of course, likes hitting objects under water, and most engines have some kind of safety device so that if a propeller does this it either stops or slips in some way. The outboard engines whose owners carry little boxes of shear-pins solve the problem by incorporating these short, round pieces of metal, which break—or, shear—when the propeller meets an obstruction.

The pin fits in a slot to lock the propeller on to the shaft which spins it round. If the propeller gets itself jammed on a polythene bag, old mattress, length of barbed wire or even a thick clump of weed the soft metal pin merely snaps, and the propeller stops, while the shaft keeps buzzing merrily round. It is a simple enough device, and must certainly have saved considerable damage to propellers, drive-shafts and even engines. But when a shear-pin snaps you need (a) another shear-pin, and (b) to exchange it with the old one.

Exchange is not always an easy job, especially if you have an engine which is too heavy to lift into the body of the boat. You need to remove a split-pin, unscrew a cone, take off the propeller, take out the pieces of the old shear-pin, put in the new one, replace the propeller, screw back the cone, and replace the split-pin (and bend it). All this often has to be done with the engine tilted up, so that you are almost standing on your head hanging over the back of the boat, with your hair

trailing in the water. Any one of the objects involved can easily be dropped in the water, and indeed, many prudent boaters even carry a spare propeller as well.

Sometimes you can do all this from the bank by lying full length on the towpath, but this usually involves swinging the bows of the boat out into everybody's way. All the same, the whole delicate operation is better than being without the use of a propeller. Many a cruise, in today's rubbish-littered canals, can be saved from a sudden end by one of these wise little boxes of shear-pins—provided you remember where you put it.

Sheep

Sheep, like cows, crop up with great frequency alongside rivers and canals, and sometimes in them. Even on the lonely Leicester summit the emptiness may be interrupted by the sight of a dog rounding up a small flock for the shepherd, and most other rural waterways now and again pass fields full of sheep. The seemingly endless thousands of cattle down the Nene occasionally give way to sheep, as at Fotheringhay with its mighty church, almost-vanished castle, and sometimes awkward bridge.

Sheep are stupid creatures. If one runs they all run, tempting your dog to follow with unhappy results. If they stroll down a slope into the water they rarely have the sense to find the same slope and walk out again. And you will sometimes see them baaing anxiously along a stretch of towpath, quite unable to find the hole in the hedge through which they came.

Skipping lambs, naturally, are part of the spring scenery for those who start their cruising early enough in the year. But there are pleasanter rural alarm clocks than the noise of their mothers calling to them.

Sowerby Bridge

All over the waterway system are places where you cannot go any further, and I mention many under TAIL-ENDS. But Sowerby Bridge perhaps deserves a special mention. It is possibly one of the least-visited tail-ends of all, especially for the flocks of Midlands and southern boaters, but it is an extremely interesting place in several ways.

For a start—though I am only a recent convert myself—no-one should really miss the cruise up the Calder & Hebble to get there. This is a fine navigation, which looks from the map as if it is entirely industrial, though in fact when you follow it you often find yourself lost among trees. And even where you touch such towns as Brighouse there are often pleasant and welcoming lengths alongside.

There are fascinating locks with an intriguing variety of bollards, barge-pole-holes and paddle-gear (with much of it worked by unusual hand-spikes, *qv*), but though the water is often wide and deep, it is only fair to say that much of it is not recommended for drinking.

All the same, the Calder & Hebble is a memorable cruise, with encouraging coal-barges along one part, a unique lift-bridge up the branch to Huddersfield, a busy basin at Dewsbury, and an especial welcome from the Calder Navigation Society all the way along. Some members may well greet you at the strange group of three locks at Salterhebble, the owest of which has that rare device (for canals)—a guillotine gate at its bottom end. The curving sweep of these three locks is a curious oasis alongside quite busy roads.

Then you are on the surprisingly remote top level, past an odd curved factory front in one place, to the basin at Sowerby Bridge. You will then see another good reason for the trip, for the old wharves and warehouses lying here below the Pennines not only show a clear past history, but offer now a bustling and developing present. For they are once more busy with boats and boat-services, and alive again compared with a few years ago.

Intriguing, too, is the fact that the disused Rochdale Canal over the moors forks off to the side of the basin. A short length is in use, but then there is a derelict lock before the canal disappears for a while. It emerges again, and you can follow it through magnificent scenery and 92 locks to Manchester—but not in a boat. With the amazing restoration of recent years, however, don't despair even of the Rochdale.

If you really want a complete change from the more usual and increasingly busy cruising grounds, a trip up the Calder & Hebble to Sowerby Bridge will certainly give it to you.

Spaghetti Junction

This name, though unofficial, is bound to pass into history for it is widely applied to a weird piece of motorway knitting which grew up at the north-east corner of Birmingham, where the passing M6 motorway had to be linked with several other roads which happened to be there already.

The connection with waterways is that already a crossroads of canals existed in the same place, and for good measure there was also a river underneath the lot. But despite this the motorway builders made themselves a mass of concrete stilts of various heights and slung up a collection of roads over the waterways. Since this was a motorway junction, the builders couldn't just join roads together and put up a lot of traffic lights. They had to fly them over and under each other, in the approved expensive

land-consuming modern fashion, and this is why the resultant interweavings threw up the obvious name 'Spaghetti'.

The result may be environmentally revolting, but it is an undoubted technical achievement. The passing motorist is almost entirely unaware of the ramifications, since he is gone in a flash, whichever route he takes. Indeed, there is nowhere where you can get a really good view of everything except perhaps from a helicopter, and even that may not show you the canals, partly under the concrete.

The view from the water is fascinating, even if far from complete. Coming from Fazeley you run alongside the elevated M6 for some time as a sort of hors d'oeuvre, and then you begin to have a fair idea of the flyovers and flyunders ahead of you as you notice snatches of traffic at different levels, and collections of concrete stilts of different heights. But you have to take your

118

eye away from this to decide on your own choice of route. It is a simpler choice than the cars have, but as the concrete cover begins you must make up your mind.

A sharp first left would take you down the Grand Union without touching the centre of Birmingham. More or less straight on, among gloomy pillars, the Tame Valley Canal takes you on a sweep northwards round the Black Country. Or fork second left to continue along the Birmingham & Fazeley up the astonishing Aston/Farmers Bridge lock-way into Birmingham (qv).

Cruising was an incredible experience when they were building the road junctions, since temporary bridges had to be removed by crane whenever a boat came along. But now, if you ignore the forest of legs, you are almost entirely unaware of the traffic roaring in all directions above you. It seems impossible that waterways under a motorway exchange can be peaceful, but they really are.

Stenson

I give this Trent & Mersey lock the place of honour as the most sadistic lock I know, especially for single-handed boaters. If you have just come through those gentle little narrow locks above Burton—Tatenhill, Branston and Dallow Lane—you are in for a rude shock when you eventually reach Stenson. It is 12ft 4in deep for a start, looking like a small canyon and it is also a broad lock, the first of the remaining six on the canal.

So you set about it. Its first trick is for a top gate to swing gently open again after you have closed it, and before you have been able to start on the bottom paddles. In any case, you cannot do this in a hurry, if at all, for the bottom paddles are brutes. An ordinary windlass may well fail to start them, and I would strongly recommend a long-armed Leeds & Liverpool type. You will certainly feel like a rest as the mass of water empties itself. But watch that your propeller does not hook up on the huge cill.

Strength back, you will need it to open the bottom gates, for their massive arms are on the short side. Then you discover that this monster has the all-too-common Trent & Mersey trick of having no towpath under the bridge. If you are on your own, or everyone has got off the boat in horror or merely to help, you consider getting back on again in order to get the boat out of the lock. But this is no light-hearted leap, with your roof over 6ft below, and tending to drift away across the lock anyhow. So you pull the boat up to the wall and descend a vertical ladder rather rapidly before the boat drifts again, with your ropes in your teeth and your windlass in your hand.

If this descent doesn't appeal, you try the 'heave-and-run-across' trick. This consists of standing in the middle of the bridge below the lock and giving a mighty pull on your rope to get the boat moving under the bridge and out of the lock. You drop the rope on it and dash across the bridge, just as most of Derby's commuters are going home. By the time you've shinned down a steep set of slippery steps the boat should be emerging if the wind hasn't blown it back. But since it is a broad lock, and there is a weir coming out just there, the chances are that the boat is across the canal out of reach. So you wish you had remembered to bring your long shaft off the boat in the first place, to catch it.

The last time I was there, as if to emphasise its sadistic habits, one of Stenson's top paddles threw a water-spout up my trouser-leg. So all in all, no marks out of ten for Stenson.

Stop locks

Among the many varieties of locks, those called stop locks are as odd as any. Some are not really locks at all, since they no longer have gates, or the gates are permanently open. The almost-gateless one at the beginning of the Ashby Canal, and the open-guillotined one at the top of the Stratford are examples of locks which aren't.

Elsewhere—Autherley, Hawkesbury and Hall Green for example—there are locks to be worked, but the water-level changes no more than a few inches. This is really the clue to the

Stop lock—Hawkesbury

Tail-end: Preston

existence of these structures for they were built where one canal company's waterway met that of another, and one or both companies hated passing a drop of water or a boat without keeping track of it. So the locks were built both to control the water and to catch the boats and take their tolls.

Toll houses and perhaps lock houses have gone now, and where the two waterways are level the lock gates have either gone or gone out of use. A slight difference in level, though, means you must still work rather absurdly through as if in a full-blown lock. And sometimes, as at Autherley, this may cause a queue as long as for a tollkeeper.

Tail-ends

Inevitably, around any inland waterway system, there will be many navigational tail-ends. No doubt originally the people living there thought of them as beginnings—the beginnings of their own vital water-link with other places. But today they are dead-ends for cruising boats, and often not visited as frequently as they might be. Yet travelling up these scattered waterways—long and short—in order to come back again is an interesting and often adventurous experience.

Take Slough, for example. The Slough Canal Group of the Grand Union Canal Society were worried that nobody tackled their 5-mile branch from the Grand Union, so they actually designed a plaque to present to boats which took the trouble to go to Slough. It is an unexpected experience, too. You turn off the GU, and at once you seem lost between high banks and trees and bushes, with plenty of flowers on them. There are flowers in the water also, both yellow and white water-lilies, which are not very common on canals.

You feel there are various horrors lurking behind these screening trees, but you see very little of them until you pass a short housing burst, complete with its deposits of easy chairs and old prams. The weed can be thick in summer, but there's usually a good channel up the middle. Vast oil-tanks appear towards the end, and you may run over discarded supermarket trolleys under one bridge, but you come to a peaceful little basin at last. There are more lilies and a timber-yard, which rashly doesn't seem to use the canal for transport. Then you can shop within a few yards and be back on the GU for lunch.

Not all tail-ends are as easy as Slough. If you want to try the one at the top of the Chesterfield you must plan your times down the Trent, with advice from Cromwell lock. You also need to ring up West Stockwith lock, and be outside its tall gates at the right time. And even when you have risen from the Trent's tides, and set out through Misterton to swing round Gringley, you have 16 locks ahead, first broad, then narrow. There are shallows and weed, but a friendly boat club to give you a hand if needed.

The far end is below Morse lock at Worksop, and used to be an unannounced mass of mud which effectively brought you to a stop. This is being tidied up now, and a decent turning-place made, with Morse lock possibly restored. The other 48 locks to Chesterfield, however, look as if they will stay for ever as they are—useless. But you never know, these days.

Then there's Aylesbury, at the end of an arm with the same number of locks as the whole of the Chesterfield, though only 6¼ miles long. But I have written more of this arm elsewhere, qv.

In complete contrast to Aylesbury try the Ashby Canal's tail-end. As opposed to being in the middle of a town, it is in the middle of nowhere. And instead of 16 locks there are no locks at all—in 22 miles at that. So you can cruise the whole canal in less time than it takes to lock down to Aylesbury.

Irises line much of the way in June, and a fair amount of weed, while getting to the side to moor is a difficult job most of the time. But there are several pleasant calling-places such as Stoke Golding and Shackerstone before the short Snarestone tunnel brings you up against the barred canal end, with the rest of it filled in. Look out for the Midland Railway boundary-posts, standing with their backs to you on the side away from the towpath in almost every field.

Of the Llangollen's tail-end perhaps the less said the better. The last few miles are fine enough, but the rest isn't a patch on the Brecon, for example. The snag about the end of the Llangollen is that you're certain to find far too many other people there as well as yourself. In the narrow, shallow length high above the town there's much chivvying and jockeying for places, reminiscent of Piccadilly Circus apart from the speed. So try the Brecon instead if you can get to it. I have written of it elsewhere in this book, and whether it is the stone-walled end in Brecon or the indeterminate silted end near Pontypool, try them, as well as the spectacular journey in between.

Like the Brecon, the Lancaster also has two tail-ends—or three if you include the Glasson branch (qv). The ends of the main line are entirely different from each other. At Tewitfield the canal is suddenly sawn off by a bridge which then also crosses the M6 alongside. So the more interesting waterway northwards has been arbitrarily blocked. But Tewitfield has been made into a surprisingly good little turning-point, peaceful despite M6, clean and fresh and tidy.

At the other end of the Lancaster, however, another decapitation has made an end in the middle of Preston, having no purpose at all—no turning-place, no building, no facilities. It is a little stub beyond the last turning-hole by Ashton Basin, so nobody ever goes up this length which is now a weedy junk-filled mess. It looks especially sad when you remember that with a bit of luck the canal ought to have crossed the River Ribble, as it crosses the Lune at Lancaster, and then gone on to link the Leeds & Liverpool.

Optimistically, in fact, a southern part of the Lancaster was actually dug beyond the Ribble. But in the end it was incorporated in the Leeds & Liverpool, and now forms the stretch of that canal from Johnson's Hillock to the top of the Wigan locks. There is still a miserable bit of it pointing towards Preston.

There are many other tail-ends, of course. The upper limits of navigable rivers amount to tail-ends for boats, though not in such a brutal way as the ends of canals, for there is still a waterway beyond. But the Cam in Cambridge, the Lee fizzling out in Hertford and the Stort in Bishop's Stortford, not to mention the Thames at Lechlade, the Severn at Stourport and the Trent at the A6 by Shardlow—all are tail-ends for navigation of anything but canoes.

But I have not yet finished with 'full stop' tail-ends on canals. At Runcorn the Bridgewater now stops where locks once took it down. The Erewash has an interesting end now in the restored Great Northern Basin—though it once joined other canals. There is Market Harborough with its fine boat-building and hire base, and revived Welford with a busy yard, not to mention the end of the Peak Forest by noisy A6 and a railway, at Whaley Bridge.

Perhaps the oddest of tail-ends are in the Birmingham Canal Navigations. Many have vanished, but you can still visit the weird surroundings of Anglesey Basin in the north, with Chasewater dam above and clear water coming in. The A5 now chops off the Cannock Extension Canal at the busy narrow-boat spot at Norton Canes. There is an out-of-this-world little boatyard at a tail-end at Bumblehole, narrow boats move in the works at Coombeswood beyond Gosty Hill tunnel, and there's Bradley, where British Waterways has a yard.

But perhaps the finest BCN tail-end now is the newly-restored Titford Canal, where six locks at Oldbury take you to the highest level of all, and along a pleasant stretch where the local council has lent its aid and money. There is now a leisure area where once was junk and dereliction.

There are may other ends as I look again at the map: the abrupt end to the Ripon Canal, for example—the furthest point north on the main waterway network (see OXCLOSE); and of course the now-restored double end to the Caldon, taking you out into magnificent country from Stoke-on-Trent. There are a few little tail-ends on the Middle Level for shallow-draught boats. Not least, there are all those expanding tail-ends on the Pocklington, the Yorkshire Derwent, the Kennet & Avon, and others which are beginning to appear at the most unlikely places. Long may they continue to extend themselves.

There's one other kind of tail-end where an inland waterway reaches the sea. But you will find some of these under TIDAL LOCKS.

Three Locks

There is a great Mecca for car-borne picnickers and beer-drinkers not far north of Leighton Buzzard on the Grand Union Canal, where three locks together at Soulbury drop the canal down a slope and give their name to a pub alongside.

On a sunny weekend in August this is one of the busiest gongoozling places on the waterways, with swarms of children and adults clambering all over the gates and lining the lock-sides, so that taking a boat through is not only an embarrassing but also hazardous experience. All the problems arising from gongoozlers at locks are there threefold—the little knots round you as you wind up the paddles, the groups on the wrong side

of the balance-beams as you swing the gates open, the lines on the very edge of the lock peering down, the skipping children tripping over your ropes, 'experts' explaining the whole process to their friends, unattended (or uncontrolled) children swinging on gates, people taking your photograph, 'helpers' doing all the wrong things, and all those others asking you questions about the boat just when you are trying to remember whether you left a paddle up or not.

Often you have just come from a peaceful stretch of canal, to arrive suddenly at this scene. After the Three Locks, you set off on the next peaceful stretch with an exhausted sigh of relief.

Tidal locks

You can set out in any direction from anywhere on the main inland network and eventually reach the sea—or at least the tide coming up from the sea. Your last lap may be down a fair

Tidal lock: Tarleton

length of non-tidal river, but there are also several places where
a canal ends abruptly at a tidal estuary. At such places the inland
boater normally comes to a stop, for his boat is not built for
dealing with tides, and he probably knows nothing of them
anyhow. But tidal locks are well worth visiting, even if you
have to sit there and peer at the normally forbidden waters
beyond.

Some of these waters are, however, used by inland boats. The
Great Ouse reaches its last lock at mighty Denver Sluice, where
the tide outside rises and falls pretty thoroughly. But for half a
mile there is a fairly regular traffic to and from the two
entrances to the Middle Level. With advice from the lock-
keepers at Salters Lode and Denver, this quick dash can be done
sensibly and safely at the right time.

The Nene not far away, however, places its last lock 26 miles before the sea, and inland boats stop at Dog-in-a-Doublet (qv). The Norfolk Broads, in contrast, need no sea-lock on their way to the sea at Great Yarmouth. To most people's surprise, the Broads are officially tidal for most of their area. Oddly, however, if you visit Oulton Broad, there is a sea-lock out to Lowestoft harbour and the sea.

Still among rivers, the Thames and Trent are comparable in one respect. Both have their tidal locks a long distance inland, leaving inland boats to brave tidal journeys in order to reach other non-tidal waterways. There are no quick dashes as at Denver. The Trent has its tidal lock at Cromwell, giving you 16 tidal miles to Torksey for the Fossdyke, 31 if you want to join the Chesterfield at West Stockwith, or a long 43 to get to the Sheffield & South Yorkshire at Keadby (qv), where there can be an alarming tide. The Thames is not so bad, but you have a 5-mile trip from Teddington lock to get into the Grand Union at Brentford, or 21 more adventurous miles to lock into Limehouse Basin for the Lee or the Regent's Canal.

Tidal locks on canals include some already mentioned along the rivers: Torksey, West Stockwith and Keadby bring canals to the tidal Trent, and Brentford and Limehouse lead Grand Union branches to the tidal Thames. The tidal doors and the lock at Salters Lode bring the Middle Level out into the Great Ouse, and at one time the Wisbech Canal used to enter the tidal Nene. On the Yorkshire Ouse there are canal tidal locks at Goole and—more likely for inland boats—Selby.

The Severn is unusual. The route downriver eventually uses the Gloucester-Sharpness Ship Canal to avoid the dangerous tides of the estuary. But those tides also make themselves felt at times as far as the lock at Tewkesbury. The real tidal lock, however, is from Sharpness docks, and at times even inland cruisers use it, with enough knowledge or a pilot, to get to Avonmouth and into the Bristol Avon. But this involves an adventurous mingling with great sea-going vessels.

I have not run out of tidal locks even now. With some trouble you can leave the Shropshire Union at Chester and go through three locks into the Dee. And the fascinating Glasson

branch (qv) takes you from the Lancaster to the Lune. But the most intriguing tidal lock is perhaps that at the end of the Rufford branch of the Leeds & Liverpool. You make your way down through seven heavy locks and some awkward swing bridges—not to mention a good deal of weed perhaps—and at last you come to a tall lock over the estuary of the River Douglas, which may be a mere trickle below. You feel quite out of place among the collection of sea-going cruisers or yachts in the canal. It is a weird spot as you perch there with the river below. It could take you quickly to the Ribble, and it is a pity it cannot then take you upriver into the isolated and sawn-off Lancaster Canal at Preston.

Tractors

This is not such an unusual subject for waterways as you would think, for I have come across at least two cases of tractors pulling boats on canals in England, and on the French canals there used to be miles of rails along some towpaths, with tractors regularly acting as horses.

There is not much towing on British towpaths now, but if you find yourself wandering through the East End, for example, you might meet a towing tractor. You run down the Regent's Canal, then turn sharp left into the well-hidden entrance of the Hertford Union Canal (or Duckett's). There is only 1¼ miles of this link to the River Lee, but it has three locks, and up them at times comes a remarkable sight, a lighter full of timber on its way to a woodyard above the top lock. And pulling it in unbelievable fashion is a small tractor which looks as if it would hardly pull a small cabin cruiser. It drags this heavily-laden affair inch by inch into the locks, where the boat fits like a glove. The towrope looks flimsy as it slides over balance-beams and chafes on lock edges. At the second lock the tractor squeezes under an overhanging bridge and climbs a very steep slope to clear the beam of the lock-gate, with the lighter doing its best to drag it back and into the cut.

How long this has been going on—or even if it is still going on—I do not know, but I was unfortunate enough once to have to follow a tractor-pulled lighter through these three locks. I have never seen anything enter a lock so slowly. But then, any boat as deeply laden as that lighter, and with only the thickness of a razor-blade between it and the lock-sides, would have moved slowly, tractor or no.

I gather—but I have never caught one—that tractors also work up the Hanwell flight on the Grand Union from Brentford. This is a fine sweeping stretch of canal, with a towpath broad enough for steam-rollers as it passes the long hospital wall. Then, near the top of the locks, is that amazing three-level bridge carrying road, rail and canal—the canal being the pig-in-the-middle.

The most commonly-seen tractors on waterway cruises are those connected with farms. Their cabs move mysteriously above bridge parapets in the middle of nowhere. They drag ploughs and other strange machinery in fields, followed by huge flocks of gulls. They tow monstrous piles of hay-bales in summer, and trailers of grain in August. They slog through mud with sugar-beet around the Middle Level Drains, and I have seen them rounding up sheep elsewhere.

The boat and farming roles of tractors came together at least once a few years ago. One of the last coal-contract runs from the Midlands down the Grand Union found the red slurry of the Coventry near Nuneaton at last too much for it, and a pair of narrow boats came to a halt in the mud. It took some hours of pulling by a farm tractor to get them through this notoriously-silted length.

I seem to remember something similar happening to the then chairman of the IWA in the Middle Level once—only this was weeds rather than mud, and I rather think it was a lorry that eventually did the towing.

Trent river

This river was an obvious highway from early times, since it penetrates well into the Midlands past Nottingham and Burton-on-Trent—where barges once reached. It has always been a difficult navigation with long-drawn-out efforts to tame it; indeed its main pattern of locks was not completed until 1926, and a lock at Newark was not enlarged till 1952. In some ways the vast locks are now sad places, for their keepers may wait for weeks to see commercial traffic. But they are increasingly busy with pleasure boats in summer, the boats sitting down there like beetles in the Colorado Canyon.

The navigable Trent now officially starts at Shardlow, but the first locks are small, since the route has to go through the Beeston and Nottingham Canals before taking to the wide river again by Trent Bridge. The first lock below has a small chamber for small boats, and a barge lock, but from here on all the locks are monsters for the pleasure-boater. Two—Stoke Bardolph and Hazelford—are still worked mightily by hand, but the others—including, curiously, Gunthorpe in between the two manual locks—are worked electrically.

Sometimes you are so far down in a lock that you never even see the lock-keeper in his cabin. He communicates with you by a traffic signal to tell you to enter, and you go out when the

River Trent: Hazelford Lock

gates open, making it all very eerie.

The electric locks, with or without commercial trade, keep working until late at night, but the manual locks close at the end of the afternoon. You may work them for yourself after this, if you have the time, energy and patience. For you wind and wind away for ever at huge handles, both to raise paddles and to open gates. And in order to reach or leave your boat you must shin down or up an endless ladder in the locksides, carrying your ropes in your teeth.

The Trent lock-keepers are friendly, and especially helpful when you are locking uphill. They take your ropes in some cases, and always hold you gently against the wall by cunning use of the incoming current. The keeper at Hazelford lives on an island, and can reach land only by boat, and the one at Cromwell is a mine of advice about when and when not to emerge into the tidal section of the river.

The tidal section starts innocently enough at Cromwell itself, but it can become highly dangerous as you near the Humber. Every year people set out in absurdly unsuitable boats, without anchors, and at the wrong state of the tide. Yet with sense, proper equipment and advice, the journey to the Fossdyke, the Chesterfield, or the South Yorkshire at Keadby is perfectly feasible for inland boats.

The Trent on the whole is a lonely river below Nottingham. There are occasional pubs, often with precarious moorings, but usually only the power stations seem to accompany you, and there are few bridges. Newark is the exception, and luckily has a fine wealth of shops within a few yards of its ancient castle and the old Great North Road bridge. Stock up here whatever you do, for mooring in the tidal river at Gainsborough further down is an entirely different matter.

Vandals

This strange and widespread tribe—waterways section —includes a great variety of people. They range from little boys who spit over bridges at boats to vicious youths who smash up paddle-gear and even lock-gates. Hooligan, yobbo and other less-printable labels are also attached to them. They are not to be confused with gongoozlers, who on the whole are harmless, whereas vandals are varying degrees of nuisance.

These people rarely use waterways legitimately, but instead seem to vent some sort of anti-social spite, hatred, boredom or sheer destructiveness on them. One of their favourite activities is filling the water with junk, especially at bridges. Little vandals throw pebbles and polythene bags, while great hulking vandals stagger up with bedsteads, bicycles, cookers, television sets and even old cars.

There are even vandal firms, which stack up mountains of rubbish teetering on the banks, so that hunks of it regularly fall in. There are mounds of smashed cars, for example, in several places along canals, and the wise boater knows of them and cruises past with care. (See OLD CARS). Other firms surreptitiously pour in their old oil or surplus chemicals, or streams of silt from their quarries. And there are even vandal farmers who let their cows tread more and more mud into the water until it is only a few inches deep, or who toss in discarded drums emptied of their crop-spraying chemicals, or polythene bags emptied of their fertilisers.

Bored casual vandals rip down notices, remove bridge-numbers, tamper with paddle-gear, and fiddle about with lock-gates. More wicked ones hide behind bushes and walls and hurl stones or fire air-guns or catapults at boats. And as well as spit and handfuls of gravel dropped from bridges, I have seen great baulks of timber balanced on parapets ready to push off.

Most vandals, then, don't really belong to the waterways. But a few do. Canal cowboys (qv) in over-engined boats go thrashing along dragging in the towpath and upsetting everyone's beer, in their anxiety to steal the next lock and get to the pub. Rivers see even worse boating vandals in flashy speedboats, who seem quite unable to resist showing off within a yard of other boats. Then of course there are the transistor vandals, who not only cannot bear to part with their pop music as they cruise along, but who bring it out on deck and inflict it at full volume on everybody else.

Such boating types are few and far between, thank goodness, as are angler vandals. But here and there, even among the thousands who enjoy a quiet day's fishing, there are still a few who shake their fists at every boat, and rather more who leave their lunch wrappings behind them when they go home.

I do not know quite what we should do about vandals, for unfortunately they are a tribe of vermin by no means confined to the waterways.

Villages

When you travel along roads, especially away from the main highways, you constantly come to villages. This is because the roads themselves developed to serve those villages. But when you travel by water, you are at once struck by the fact that there are often no villages for miles—or for that matter, even houses.

Villages shun rivers because of the constant danger from flooding. Thus settlements were often built on higher ground clear of the flood plain. But canals miss villages for a different reason. They needed to follow level ground as far as possible, and therefore took little account of any villages near their route. Those that used them for transport would have their own wharves at the nearest convenient spot.

Generally speaking, then, as you cruise along a waterway, you have to search for your villages, but they are there all right. Along rivers you can often see them across the water-meadows where the land first starts to rise. The Nene especially offers you a whole string, and provides many a pleasant walk for shopping, a meal or a drink. Those near such rivers as the Trent and the Severn tend to hide behind the banks.

Along canals, too, the villages are likely to be invisible, but if you tie up at most bridges and just walk, you are pretty sure to find a village sooner or later. In the less-populated areas an Ordnance Survey map (the old one-inch or the new 1:50 000) is helpful.

This lack of regular villages on the route is sometimes disconcerting to newcomers, but the delights of searching for the hidden ones grow on you. Wormleighton, for example, is within walking distance of several bridges on the Oxford Canal; it takes you back centuries with an old manor house and a brown church and surprisingly quiet cottages. A few miles further along the canal you can cross fields to Priors Hardwick and good meals at the pub. Withnell Fold is a curious lost place on the Leeds & Liverpool, with a ghostly closed factory, and estate houses round three sides of a large square. Adderley takes some finding from the locks of that name on the Shropshire Union, and you may have to clamber along a disused railway line to reach the lonely part-closed church or a phone-box.

All over the waterways there are villages like this to search for, but not all hide themselves, and occasionally you run pleasantly by one. More often in recent years the waterside houses have laid out rockeries, sitting-out places and of course moorings, to make use of their waterway boundary. And 'by the canal', instead of putting off house seekers, now actually adds to a house's price. Local councils, too, have made use of waterside sites, so that at such places as Willington, near Derby, you can moor by a pleasant grassy area near to shops and pubs.

Talybont, on the Brecon, lies a little below the canal and offers three pubs, Alrewas has a place of its own at the beginning of this book, and Braunston used to be almost entirely a canal settlement, and is still heavily canal-orientated. Marsworth happily touches the Grand Union, and the otherwise characterless village of Benwick reserves its leafy and most picturesque part for the Middle Level Drain running there. There are Acton Trussell on the Staffs & Worcs (though spoilt by the distant M6 roar), Stoke Golding on the Ashby (try the *George & Dragon*), and of course canal-famous Shardlow on the Trent & Mersey (though parts have now turned their backs on the canal).

Whether by the waterside or giving you a little exercise to find them, many hundreds of villages offer you an enormous variety to explore. It is one of the pleasures of cruising to look at these varying collections of houses, churches, schools, pubs and shops, and even, if you're not too supermarket-minded and nervous, to try a whole new range of supplies for your galley.

Waterfalls

Boats coming on to the Severn from Diglis Basin at Worcester, or down the dog-leg from the Avon at Tewkesbury, meet alarming notices warning them of 'Waterfalls'. They occur at all the Severn locks, and with visions of small Niagaras flashing through their minds, boaters might be forgiven for not noticing whether the lock traffic-lights are red or green.

But 'waterfalls' seems to be an exclusive Severn name for what everybody else calls 'weirs'. The Severn 'waterfall' is in fact the river flowing happily on and dropping over a broad lip in its channel round the lock. And as on the Trent, if you are going downstream there is nothing to stop you going with it. But if the water is high and fast you ought not to be out there at all.

Fortunately the correct channel to the lock is clearly shown, and you can drop down and eventually have a look at the waterfall from its lower end. Its top is like a smooth line of stainless steel in the sun, but at its foot there is a bouncing, whirling and frothing of tumbled water, which seems to have a particular fascination for people in small boats. No doubt they are safe enough below if they do not get too near, and it looks as if the feet of these wide, foaming waterfalls are good places for fish.

Waterways Witch

This is no weird lady haunting a gloomy tunnel, but the name given to a strange contraption which you may meet in the north-west. The first one that I came across was then called *Water Witch*, and had been hired from a Bootle firm to work along the Leeds & Liverpool Canal. It was a sort of short tug, with what appeared to be an old bedstead fastened to the front. The bedstead was lowered into the water and the whole contraption moved along scooping up weed, which certainly needed dealing with in those parts. When the bedstead was full, the boat—if I can call it such—moved to the side of the canal and dumped the weed there, where it presumably rotted away.

I am partly guessing at the operation from the evidence I saw, since I always seemed to pass the *Witch* during tea-breaks. But British Waterways must have been pleased by its work, for more recently I have met a newer version in their own colours, called *Waterways Witch I*. It was on the Lancaster Canal this time, resting from its labours at Galgate, but it appears designed to do the same scoop-and-dump job as the one I saw on the L & L.

I sometimes wonder if I have dreamt all this, or if I have got the whole thing wrong, and some witch has cast a spell on me. For I do not remember ever seeing pictures of these gadgets anywhere, or hearing or reading a word about them from anyone else. But surely my camera, too, can't have been bewitched?

Wolverhampton Flight

Most people talk of Tardebigge, Hatton and Wigan when the discussion turns to flights of locks. And of course Wigan and Hatton in particular deserve to be talked about, being quite tough propositions. Wigan easily leads the way in variety of paddle-gear, awkward lock-ladders, boisterousness of gate-paddle-torrents, and general memorableness as you climb up to a magnificent view over Wigan itself.

Hatton, once you've got the swing of its unusual paddles, begins to get monotonous; and Tardebigge is much gentler than the other two, though it seems to go on for ever—especially when you realise that the so-called 30 locks are in fact 42. But the flight that most people forget to mention is Wolverhampton, possibly because there is still a feeling around that you can cruise all over the canal system so long as you don't go near the Birmingham Canal Navigations. And the Wolverhampton 21 take you, with a vengeance, slap into this weird network of waterways.

They are narrow locks and easy enough; their fascination really consists of the way they start so surreptitiously among trees and bushes and fields from the Staffs & Worcs, and pop you out at the end among one of the few grim areas of the whole BCN.

You can easily miss Aldersley Junction, on the opposite side of the S&W only half a mile from the much busier, similarly-named, Autherley Junction, where the Shropshire Union takes off. But Aldersley hides under an old brick bridge, which many people pass without realising that it is one of the BCN gateways. Yet you can pass deep rope-grooves in the bridge-corner, go up well-worn stone steps, and there is the first lock of the flight.

The pile of locks ahead is not obvious at first, for the next one is some distance away. This second lock, too, is unusual in that it has a single gate at the bottom instead of the usual pair—though the two gate-paddles have to be worked from opposite sides. Its top ground-paddles, in addition, lean in drunken fashion reminiscent of the Huddersfield Narrow Canal. It was in fact built as an afterthought to the original 20.

The gentle introduction to Wolverhampton continues as you pass the racecourse, and alongside one lock I once met half-a-dozen pigs snoring in the shade. But the massive railway viaduct heralds the beginning of the built-up area, though there are still a few stretches of open ground to come. Railways and factories press in, however, especially on your right, though the locks now get so thick that you have little time to gaze around.

Don't miss, though, the fine-carved numbers and dates on some lock-shoulders, and a rusty old name or two still clinging to little bridges. Then alongside the top lock is a typical example of BCN lock-house, foursquare and solid, with the metal number-plates that you see all over the BCN.

You shoot out of the flight at last, with more railways and a builder's yard, past an iron BCN towpath bridge through a canyon of high brick walls. On the left is an uninviting square opening, and unless you are due along the main line at Farmers Bridge in Birmingham, try diving through the hole. It will take you sweeping round on the Wyrley & Essington Canal, which has some of the best calling-places on the whole warren of Navigations.

So next time you find yourself down the Staffs & Worcs don't pass by the Wolverhampton flight. It may not be as magnificent as some, but it is a worthwhile exercise. And the pigs may still be there.

Working parties

Almost every canal society or trust, every IWA branch, and many boating clubs have one important member whose job it is to organise working parties. That is, he rustles up members who will give up weekends and maybe travel long distances to work

Worm gear: Leeds & Liverpool

like slaves on derelict locks, cluttered-up channels and overgrown towpaths. Some organisers, indeed, feel that this is the be-all and end-all of the existence of their society, branch or club, and tend to hint that members who do not get themselves knee-deep in mud really ought to be thrown out.

There are of course other ways of helping the waterway cause, but undoubtedly the working parties supplied by groups all over the country have had a great effect on authorities and public attitudes wherever there is a waterway. For more on this fascinating movement, however, see NAVVIES.

Worm gears

Most of the 57 varieties of gear provided for opening paddles at locks use straightforward cogs. Either there are cogwheels of different sizes meshing teeth with each other and with an

Worm Gear: Hatton

upright rack to lift the paddle-shutter; or as on the Leeds & Liverpool (and surprisingly at Saul alongside the Gloucester-Sharpness), your cog moves a horizontal rack of teeth to slide a scissor-board sideways.

But as a change from the permutations of cogs and racks, you occasionally find grease-covered twirling worms instead of racks. The most clearly-seen example of this is again a Leeds & Liverpool speciality. The worm part is upright, and is turned either by a handle at the top moved horizontally instead of the more usual vertically, or by a two-armed capstan to be spun, as on an old-fashioned metal press. As the worm turns, a gadget slides up it, and pulls up the rod connected to the paddle-shutter far below. Some of the L&L paddles of this type are at the very edge of the lock and you must lean precariously out to see if the thing is working.

On the northern part of the Grand Union which was remodelled in the 1930s there are ranks of worm-driven paddles—a particularly striking sight up the Hatton flight. The gear is enclosed in leaning casings, however, and you have to peer through a little hole to see it.

I have vague memories of odd bits of worm-gear elsewhere usually at derelict locks (but isn't that one at Welches Dam?) And there have also been experimental gears around the canal at various times, some obviously worm-driven, but all with their works mysteriously hidden from our inquisitive gazes.

Zoo

Let us take finally a gentle trip from Little Venice, near the heart of London, along the Regents Canal. You can do this on a variety of trip boats if you wish, and after a tree-lined stretch among fine houses you pass through Maida Hill tunnel, then under the tracks leading to Marylebone Station, until by a surprising gentle wooded cutting, suddenly you find yourself in the middle of London Zoo.

You cannot get in from the canal except off a Zoo water-bus but you get a free look at Lord Snowdon's aviary above the towpath side, and opposite this are various humpish animals who look disdainfully down at you. I thought also that I caught sight of the top end of a giraffe one day, but I couldn't be sure.

This stretch of central London canal is certainly astonishing and unexpected and, despite the occasional heavy wash from a Zoo boat, the greenery, the relaxed people on the towpath, and the unusual bonus of the Zoo itself provide a memorable waterway length. Don't be too distracted, however, to miss the sharp left turn at the end, which takes you to the rather less rural realities of the locks and the canal on its way to Limehouse.